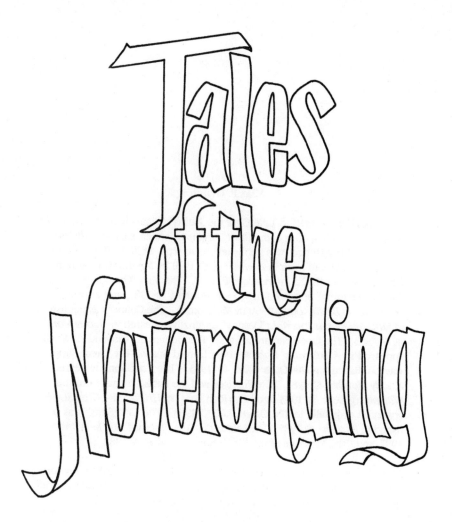

Tales of the Neverending

Mark Littleton

MOODY PRESS
CHICAGO

*To Grandpop Littleton,
who first taught me the magic of story*

Contents

Ends

Beginnings

1
A Fantastic Decision

I've thought about it for years, but only recently did I begin to grasp it. I'd like to say it all came in a flash, or a dream—even a vision. But frankly, I'm not sure He would communicate it that way. Just the same, the experience changed me. Or perhaps I should call it insight.

No, it was more than an insight.

Well, not to quibble. Let me simply tell you what it was. You be the judge.

The issue was creation. You, me, all of us from all time. Angels. Demons. Amoebas, giraffes, houseflies, skunks, the whole shootin' match, as some say. What concerned me was not just creation though. It was why. Why He took the trouble. Why He did it, knowing what would happen—evil and all. It seemed incredible. That is, unless He didn't happen to know that evil would wreck everything. But of course I can't believe that. He's omniscient. Knows everything that is, was, and will be. Every possibility. I once heard a preacher say He knew what each of us would be like—whether brown hair and blue eyes, red hair and green eyes, or blond hair and brown eyes. He knows every combination. He knew what would have happened if I were born in the first century or the twenty-first.

Knows all the details, too. The number of hairs on my head. Every one! I wonder if each has a number. Or a name. Why does He go to such trouble?

Of course, it's not any trouble for Him. He just knows. Instantly. He's simply aware of it at any given moment. It doesn't take Him the least effort. No research. No magnifying glasses. No work. It's stupendous. But I'm getting away from the issue. This is what happened.

I imagined myself going to Him. To the throne room, I mean. Right into the holy place. (Understand, I know under normal conditions no one could even glance at His face. But these aren't normal conditions.)

Anyway, I was there in the throne room—a sort of adviser. (I know that's crazy, me an adviser to the Lord! But it was only in my imagination. I was trying to get a firmer hold on something, something important to me, to all of us.) I imagined that I was there at the beginning, before anything was, before He'd even begun the first act of creation. We were talking about the possibility of creating majestic beings like Himself. He called them "angels."

At the same time that I was there, I already knew everything I know now. (That's why I was an adviser.) I was there to consult with Him about whether it was worth it to create these creatures, in light of the risk.

He told me about His plan. "But, Lord," I said, "You know that if You create these angels, one of them will rebel and lead one-third of them in war against You." He nodded and told me He knew it all.

"Why create them, then, if they're going to cause so much trouble?" I asked.

He told me we were getting ahead of things. He wanted to spell it all out before we decided.

He informed me that after the rebellion of these angels, He would create a whole universe and another set of beings called "humans" (of which I was one, as you know). They would be even more incredible than the angels because they would be "in His image," reflections of His character and nature. Only, they would be on a lower scale since they'd be more confined—fixed in time and space. (You know about this, too, so I needn't go into it.)

Of course, by now I was upset. I already knew precisely what would happen: the second rebellion. In a flash I saw the

12

billions on planet Earth kicking and hating, killing and maligning, gossiping and reviling. I began to shake. He asked me what was wrong.

I said, "Lord, don't You know that shortly after You create the first humans they also will rebel against You, turn Your world into a place of havoc and despair, revile You to Your face, and hate You? Haven't You considered the carnage they'll turn Your universe into?" He nodded, and for the first time His face whitened.

I shuddered. I thought He might weep. But He didn't. He composed Himself and told me He knew all that would happen. Every detail. He explained that these people made in His image would spit on one another and steal and lie and kill and cheat. Twice He closed His eyes as though in pain, but He assured me He knew all of it.

I couldn't restrain myself. He didn't seem to be considering the real impact of these things. I cried, "Lord, You can't create them like that. You'll have to make it impossible for them to rebel. It'll only be pain, forever and ever. Your own heart will be crushed within You. Please stop this before it goes too far."

He gazed at me and took a breath. I waited quietly. He didn't speak for a long time. Finally, He said, "Do you suggest that I create an inferior being then, one without My sacred mark upon it, one without the fullness of My image?"

For the first time I felt uncomfortable. I said, "Perhaps You can just dispense with the test in the Garden, the freedom to choose good over evil. Maybe if they weren't tested, it would work out. Somehow."

He replied that that was impossible, for that was the very thing that made them most like Him. Furthermore, He said He planned to make plenty of such choiceless creatures to populate the world and be the servants of the humans. But the humans would be as like Him as it is possible for a creature to be like its Creator. No facet of His nature could be held back. He would create a perfect reflection.

I said nothing, but my heart despaired. It appeared that He would forge ahead with this, regardless of the suffering involved.

13

He told me of His other plans—how He planned to redeem the humans through a series of steps, culminating in a sacrifice that He Himself would make.

Of course, I knew instantly what He referred to. I said, "Lord, You're speaking of the suffering and death of Your Son, Your only Son, who is as much a part of Your being as the human heart is of man's."

He nodded and closed His eyes. For the first time a tear glinted there.

This was too much for me. I felt weak. I wanted to shake Him, to tell Him no. It was too much pain, too high a cost.

I said, "Lord, You are aware that the Son will die on a cross, the most torturous form of execution these rebellious humans will devise in their hatred of You. You know that they will hate Him and curse Him through the ages. They will trample His name, and the few who do believe in Him will be driven from the planet like rats from a beach. You know that in the moment He dies He will be separated from You and will suffer a pain greater than all the anguish and agony of all men for all time in hell. You realize what He will pay if You create? And what You Yourself will pay?"

I was angry. I thought He didn't understand. For certain He'd gone too far, hadn't considered the immensity of this suffering.

But as I gazed at Him, His whole body shook, and suddenly great heaves racked Him. I knew now how it hurt Him even to think of His Son's suffering. I felt a great compassion for Him. I said quietly, "Lord, You do not have to take this step. Nothing has yet been created. At the risk of preventing even my existence, I have to say to You that the cost and the pain are too great. Think of it—You and Your beloved Son separated, bearing the penalty of billions of souls who are born without caring for You or for Him."

He was looking at me, penetrating me to the heart.

I turned away. I felt the heat and fire of His own life touching mine. Nonetheless, I continued, "Lord, there's still time. You don't have to create. You can make some other world, some other universe, one that will do only as You desire."

He continued looking at me, kindly, understanding. It was not an angry gaze but plaintive, almost sympathetic. Finally, He said, "Such a world, as we already discussed, would be useless to anyone."

I cried, "Then don't create at all, Lord. Give up this dream. There's no point."

He shook His head. "No. There is something you have forgotten."

I waited.

"If I don't create such a world, I will never do the very thing for which I am who I am—a creator. A creator must create. It is his nature."

I thought about this. "But You are also love and grace and goodness and justice. What about these?"

"Even they are useless characteristics unless they have some way of manifesting themselves."

I thought hard. I still believed He was not yet given to this. I could dissuade Him.

But He said, "You have forgotten something else."

It seemed that His great form trembled again.

"Is not fellowship important?" He said. "Isn't what you have in Me important to you? Do you not think that the price of My own personal pain is worth the value of love, understanding, and a kinship of souls?"

"Yes, for us," I admitted. "But You do not need it, Lord. You can exist without it."

He smiled. "Of course. But what if I don't want to? What if I must put the needs of My creatures higher than My own?"

I swallowed. I was astonished. This was getting more difficult than I had imagined.

"When you were down there building your house, was it worth the creation of the house to smash your thumb a few times?"

I looked down. "I suppose."

He seemed to be looking far off. I knew there was something else springing within His heart, and I burned to hear it.

A great tear fell from His eye, but He didn't speak, and I waited a long time, saying nothing myself. Partly out of fear. Partly out of reverence. And partly—no, mainly—because this was what I had come for. This was the revelation I had longed to understand.

"If I create," He said, "there will be much pain for all concerned. All of us will suffer. But . . ." He paused and looked at His hands. I saw the traces of white on them. Scars. "But I will make a way for men to find redemption and hope in the midst of their pain."

I blanched. "The cross" rang in my mind again.

"In making that redemption, I will pay an ultimate price, a price which even I shrink from paying."

I nodded. That was precisely the reason I wanted Him not to do it.

"But," He continued, "does a brave man shrink from doing what is right even if it costs him his life?"

He looked at me, eyes gentle and pained, but kind and joyous.

I couldn't speak.

He smiled, the shy, brave smile of a person who must give all in order that another might live. "This is something I want to do, this sacrifice."

"Just to do it?" I said, confused. It seemed almost self-satisfying.

"No," He said with a wistful look. "Not just to satisfy Myself. That would be pure selfishness. No, I want to do it because . . . "

I waited again. I could see no reason good enough. What could it be? I gazed into His eyes. Somehow I saw in them all the centuries of angelic and human battle against Him. I saw the arrows of hatred piercing His heart. I could feel the swords of rejection and malice cutting great gashes in His soul. I saw all the hatred and agony accumulated and nailing His heart to that cross. I could see the faces of those who had rejected Him, their voices rising up in accusation against Him. The horror was so great I flinched and turned away.

But something drew me back.

I looked again, and this time I saw something deeper. I saw the Son rising. I saw Him triumphant. I saw Him defeating those enemies and embracing those who loved Him. I could see them flying into His arms like wives into the arms of husbands returning alive from battle.

I saw His kingdom, too glorious to fathom. I saw the Son reigning, the Father above it all, reveling in the joy of His creation. And I saw His creatures: a mother with a child at her breast, a young man offering a rose to his love, a pastor with tears in his eyes greeting his father newly risen and alive. I saw them all—billions singing the amazing graces of Zion, climbing the mountains of His love. I saw them climbing, ruling the world with perfect justice and righteousness. Never again a murder. Never again a cheat. Never again a loss or a forced entry or a broken bone or a firing squad, destroying a hundred lives with the flick of a trigger. I heard the songs of Zion rising up in throats almost too taut with joy, yet too full not to sing. I saw them drawing near Him, basking in His beauty and light.

And I saw myself. My family. My people. My daughter and son and great granddaughter.

I saw us—Him and me—walking, talking, joking, laughing, running together, racing, climbing the mountains of His holiness together. I saw Him and me, sharing a daffodil, inspecting the petals, reveling in the beauty. I saw us, traveling the galaxies, watching the light refract through the jewels of His kingdom and coming away, choked up in the crush of it all. I saw both of us standing among lions, galloping together on stallions white as snow, and flying on the wings of eagles. I saw us embracing and laughing and swimming the vast oceans, racing to see who would win this time. I saw us, our hearts knit together in such a love that no sword, no deception, no demon, no rain of hail, or darkness of night could dispel it.

I was almost too stunned to speak. My heart seemed so full I thought it would burst.

Then I saw one thing more: Him. His heart. Suddenly, I saw the marrow of His soul, the glory of His character. I saw the depth and height and length and breadth of that love and grace that would sacrifice all—His life and blood—that I might live. I saw how He took me from dust to flesh to everlasting spirit. I saw how He came to me in my degraded shack, where I was swilling my drugs, cursing my parentage, and hating my wife—and turned me back. I saw Him speak in tender words, waiting patiently through my years of anger and bitterness, faithfully wooing and seeking me without a single demand upon my soul, except that I believe He loved me.

I saw how He transformed me from a wastrel to an eternal wonder, from a horror to an honor among all creation, from mere man to the image of Himself. And I saw myself reigning with Him forever and ever. A prince. A king. A man after His own heart. One for whom He died.

"Do you understand?" He said quietly.

I nodded, my throat too constricted to speak. Suddenly, I loved Him with an intensity I had never before known. With joy, I bowed in worship before Him and sang the songs of Zion.

Then as suddenly, I found myself crying, "Oh Lord, forgive me. You are far greater than I ever imagined. Teach me more about You. Teach me everything. Hold nothing back. Show me Your full character and majesty."

His eyes smiled that great, fatherly smile of one who loves so greatly that He will do anything to make your highest joy possible. He said, "I will show you."

As joy surged through me again, I wept and looked into His face. I said, "Lord, I want to be like You. Teach me to love as You love."

He said quietly, "I will."

I fell into His arms, overcome.

And then I found myself here.

As I said at the start, I can't be sure that everything here is correct. It was only an insight, a musing. But I had to tell you. For His sake. Because He is worthy. Because He is a wonder far greater than I ever knew.

Because He is love itself. And light. And perfection.

But now I must go. He and I must meet again. We do every day now. Would you like to come along? He invites you, too, all of us. His heart is so great, He can love each of us as though we were the only one.

Anyway, thanks for listening. I had to tell it. There's no other way. He is simply too ...

Well, come now, and you will see it, too. Then you can supply the correct word.

2
The Grand Experiment

It was to be the greatest orchestra in creation. Magnificent beyond words. Beyond even the music itself. The best musicians. The most glorious pieces to play and perform. A flawless, creative, and masterful conductor.

And of course, the most appreciative audience ever: the owner, his son, and the great uncle. They had conceived it. Now they would create it instrument by instrument, musician by musician, piece by piece, performance by performance. They would do it.

And why? For nothing less than glory. Sublime, perfect, ineffable glory. Forever and ever.

The owner set about his work. He, the son, and the great uncle laid it all out. A blueprint. The grand idea fixed itself in all three minds as though in one.

They built the stage, a marvelous stratification of hues and jewels—chrysolite, ebony, sapphire, ruby, diamond—so that light filtered through and illumined each note. Effortlessly, they set the music in sublime profundity.

Three seats stood before the stage like three thrones. But the owner did not think of them as thrones so much as a place to reap the rich reward of creation's greatest melodies and harmonies.

The son took charge of the instruments, each a marvelous blending of wood, metal, jewel, fabric, string, leather, and wind. There would be myriads of each type and myriads of the myriads. Each was the masterful product of a skilled craftsman, the son himself.

The great uncle composed the music. The pieces combined every musical note, tone, chord, arrangement, riff, pitch, and modulation imaginable—compositions so varied, flawless, beautiful, new, and inexplicable that the musicians themselves would burn to perform during every waking moment.

The owner took special care of the development of the musicians—their nurture, study, and expansion—until they performed effortlessly and with perfection beyond words. The music could be nothing less than the product of myriads of hearts, souls, minds, and strengths united in one vast symphony.

The conductor himself received the benefits of the mental and spiritual acumen of all three. For years on end they labored to hone and polish him until he shone upon his podium like the sun. As he moved, light refracted from his garments like the music itself. Perfect. Beautiful.

Finally, all was ready.

The conductor stood at the podium. Multicolored light leaped from his arms, his head. All was quiet as the last moment before dawn. Then he raised his baton. Every musician stood poised to burst forth with that first vibrant allegro.

Then he let go. The music carried you to heights and depths never before experienced. The owner leaned back, astonished and grateful. A tear fell from his eye as he listened. It was his greatest moment.

For days on end they played, the orchestrations punctuated by sharp romps of individual and small group performance. Different musicians worked together with the conductor. For them the owner created special compositions, music like starlight and dawn, orchid and rose—pieces that thrilled the son and the great uncle to the dividing of heart and soul.

The joy of performance was so great that none in the whole orchestra tired for a moment. Even when a duet, trio, quartet, or soloist made a special performance, it was the gathered company—all playing and rising to the highest of crescendos as they entered into the arrangement with abandon

21

—who began to worship and enjoy the fellowship like wind through fir, or pure water gently rolling down a rock-strewn cut through the heart of a mountain.

The owner, his son, and the great uncle could not have been more pleased.

But few things in creation go on perfectly forever, and even this august gathering suffered a fracture. Almost imperceptible at first, it was unnameable, ghastly as rotten flesh.

Of course, the owner knew. From the start. So did the son and the great uncle. But it dragged at their hearts.

It was the conductor. No one in the orchestra questioned his position of authority or his intellect or his choices for the time and arrangement of each performance. No one questioned his integrity. Or his perfection. Or his right to silence one and give another the first place. Their eyes fixed on him in a calm willingness to follow.

But they all knew for whom they performed. They knew that ultimately even the conductor was an employee. And that was where the irk arose. "Employee." Some even dared to whisper the word *servant*. Never to his face. For they all knew that if he was "servant," they were something even less.

Of course, the owner never spoke in such terms. His words had a more majestic ring. "Covering cherub." "Anointed seraph." "Angel." "Principality." "Power."

But somehow "servant" cut its way into the conductor's conversation like an edged knife. He never said anything to the owner. Just dropped a hint here, a thought there.

"Does it ever cross your mind that...?"

"Do you ever think about the fact that...?"

"Have you ever considered the possibility of...?"

The conductor was such a dignified presence that no one dared question his motives. It was thought to be a mere mistake, some faulty tuning of a violin that simply needed to be gently corrected.

This the owner sought to do. He spent long sessions quietly talking with the conductor. It served as both fatherly advice and a warning. "This course you are setting yourself on," the owner said. "Do you understand that it ends in death?"

The conductor only turned away, sullen. He spoke of "freedom," and "doing what he wanted to do," and "finding his own way."

The owner said that he would find such things in time, as he learned to completely express his gifts. "Freedom," he said, "is doing what is right and best, not what you wish."

The conductor only scowled.

Soon it began to infiltrate the music. He purposely switched harmonies on some pieces, changed a melody here and there, made demands on the musicians that even the owner didn't raise. Of course, his changes grated on the beauty of the music. It was nearly ruined by the strokes he put in.

At first these changes were nearly imperceptible even to best of the musicians. And it was done all in the name of a better performance.

But the performances were not better. They were marred by the conductor's criticism, his antagonistic attitude. Soon it was plain. The conductor hated the owner.

Repeatedly, the owner warned him. "Please think long and hard about what you're doing and saying. It won't help you or anyone else." And, "You do understand that if this continues I will have to take action."

The conductor only sneered behind his back.

The owner decided to relax his rein a little more and to give the conductor more room to "find his way," as he said. But the conductor kept pushing for more.

Soon, it was clear: he didn't just want freedom to perform or do as he pleased. He wanted nothing to do with the owner. In fact, he wanted to take the owner's place completely. It was a startling revelation.

The owner, his son, and the great uncle talked long hours into the day and night. They knew what the end was. The conductor seemed bent on his course. And they knew that short of destruction or elimination, he wouldn't listen to their pleas.

Then the conductor switched tacks. He became a model director, doling out the music perfectly, though mechanically. Many thought that a real change had occurred. The conductor had found the right way. His previous fits were just missed notes in an otherwise perfect rendition of the owner's work.

But the joy was gone. The perfection remained, but the heart had been cut out. Performing had become a chore.

Yes, some played with all their hearts. But to see so many so angry, blowing and bowing and plucking their perfect notes with such virulence, tore the soul out of the music.

The conductor had a perfect explanation for the musicians who approached him about the problem. "The owner requires preposterous things of me." He gave his spiel over and over. "The owner doesn't know what he's talking about." "The owner is no musician"—unlike himself, of course. "The owner has taken too hard a hand. No freedom for anyone."

Soon, questions were flying. The conductor had ready answers. "We can form our own orchestra. We can play what we want." To each musician he privately promised special rewards. "First violinist." "First trombone." "First cellist." "The seat closest to the front." "A chance to compose and perform your own music."

The whole orchestra buzzed with talk about some "major changes." Some considered it dead wrong and hoped the owner would do something soon. But others weren't sure. What the conductor said seemed plausible, even attractive.

It was then that several of the loyal musicians went to the owner. Did he know what was happening? Had he seen the change? Was he aware of the criticism going on behind his back?

He knew.

They were astonished. "What are you going to do about it?"

He said he was working on it. Not to worry.

But it all dragged at the owner's heart, and he had many more conferences with the son and the great uncle. Finally, a meeting was called. The owner gave a speech. Musicianship. Getting back to basics. Commitment. The joy of excellence. Performance.

Everyone listened raptly. It seemed to be back to the old order. Many were content.

But the conductor went back to his manipulating between the performances. He spoke to each performer in corners, back rooms, behind the stage. It was soon clear who had taken his side and who had taken the owner's. "What do we do?" one of them asked at a special secret meeting of the New Order, as they called themselves.

"I say we take him," said the conductor. Flat. Straight out.

Some gasped and left. Others were all for it. Nearly a third of the orchestra had joined him.

"Look at him," said the conductor. "Compare him to me. Look at the son. Or that old uncle. Don't you think we can take them? It'll be over in a minute. One solid crack to the jaw, and he's done."

It was true. Neither the owner, the son, or the great uncle looked anything like the conductor or even most of the musicians. True, when they walked into the assembly, the whole place lit up. But it was the orchestra that danced the dance of light. Not them. They, in fact, were hardly noticeable. Even rumpled looking.

The conductor decided to bring it off. He and his cohorts laid out elaborate plans. Secret missions went on. They spent long sessions arguing with opposing musicians, trying to win them over.

Strangely, the owner said nothing. He seemed to be merely waiting for something to happen. So also the son and the great uncle.

It was all planned. At an evening's performance, on a certain note, every member of the New Order would jump up with his weapon—an instrument, a sharpened jewel, a chair—and dispatch the specific two or three he most hated. Everyone had an assignment.

That evening the performance was better than usual. The notes and melodies rang out with a precision not witnessed in some time.

But suddenly, at the height of one andante, the conductor turned on his podium, made a sweep with his baton, and jumped at the owner. The baton suddenly transformed into a sword of light. He struck at the owner's throat.

Instantly, the whole stage became a boiling cauldron of anger. Musicians hurled instruments and chairs, gnashed teeth, flailed away with knives and clubs. Private scores were being settled. Battles raged all over the platform. Even the owner seemed to have some trouble fending off the enraged conductor and his specially selected henchmen.

But in the end, a dividing line rose between them, and the two groups stood on either side, taunting, yelling, and panting. Most of the instruments were broken, unusable. The stage was a mess, though amazingly no one had died, and the owner himself, the son, and the great uncle had escaped harm.

As the two forces stood panting and shrieking, the owner called for silence. He stood in their midst, facing the conductor and the opposing forces behind him. "So you have chosen to rebel and fight?"

The conductor nodded, saliva and blood dripping from his chin. "We just want our own place, our own orchestra. To do as we please. We don't want to perform for you any longer."

"Why should I grant this?" asked the owner, coolly calm.

The conductor laughed. "You don't grant it. We take it."

The owner chewed his lip. "And if I let you live, what will you do?"

"First, we'll get rid of you permanently!" shouted someone behind the conductor. But the conductor waved for silence.

"We'll play our own music."

"You won't bother the group that remains loyal to me?"

"No," said the conductor. "We'll mind our own business."

"So be it," said the owner. "We shall see what you do. But you are not to play here."

A gasp went up from those with him. But a cheer rose from the group who supported the conductor. A place was agreed upon for the conductor and his group to perform to their own satisfaction. The two groups parted.

In the course of time, the owner gave all the loyalists new instruments and new music. They played beautifully.

But the conductor and his musicians had a problem. No one could compose. No one possessed skill to fashion an instrument. They couldn't play a note. Furthermore, they had no stage.

Then the conductor came up with a plan. He organized his musicians into gangs and began attacking lone musicians, invading quarters, and stealing. Many of the musicians loyal to the owner were harmed, lost their instruments, and had their fingers or lips smashed. Although the owner was able to heal their wounds, it was apparent that these incidents of injury and loss were creating serious deterioration in his orchestra. Some musicians were even turning against him.

Then it was learned that the conductor intended to take the stage and whatever instruments remained and to do his best to destroy the owner and all that now belonged to him. Now a decision had to be made, final action taken.

The owner gathered the loyalists, the son, and the great uncle together. "We have reached a point of no return. We cannot let things go on as they are. The conductor and his people are attacking and hurting ours mercilessly. We have to decide what to do."

"Can you just get rid of them altogether?" asked one of the musicians who had been brutally battered the night before, losing a precious violin in the process.

"Yes," said the owner. "I can eliminate them entirely."

The whole group gasped as one. "You can?" shouted one.

"Then why haven't you?" asked another.

"I want to discuss the options," said the owner. "So that you understand. One is that I eliminate them entirely."

"Bravo!" rang from the galleries.

The owner paced before them. "But it is not an option without its difficulties," he said. "For instance, who's to say I won't appoint another conductor who will do the same as this first one has done? We could go on and on like this for years until your numbers are so depleted we wouldn't even have an orchestra."

Everyone was silent.

27

Then someone else said, "Banish them! Send them somewhere else. Give them their own place."

The owner nodded. "That's a legitimate thought. But we have already tried that, and it hasn't worked. They do not have the power to create as I do, so they must get their own music, instruments, and place to perform by theft, trickery, and murder."

That was all true.

But the owner went on. "Anyway, don't I have a responsibility to those over there? Even though they've rejected me, I hear they're already fighting among themselves. Soon there will be splinter groups there, too. In no time they'll all be asking for their own places, their own orchestras. It could go on and on like this forever."

The group stared ahead dejectedly. Then someone said, "Why not give them another chance to come back?"

This time the son spoke up. "We've already given them that chance. They don't want it."

"Maybe in time they will," said the same musician.

"Perhaps. But how long are we to wait?" asked the great uncle. "How many of our people are hurt and maimed?"

There seemed to be no way.

But the owner looked over the group. "I will now tell you what I have decided to do. My plan is not without its hazards—for all of us. But my goal is that in the end you will all see that I am indeed worthy of the loyalty you have already shown me. I am grateful for that. And I promise I won't misuse it."

He paused, and someone said, "What are you going to do, sir?"

"We will let them make their own way—for the time being," said the owner.

"But that means they'll be attacking us in their hit squads!" shouted another.

The owner shook his head. "No, I'll see that that stops. But we will let them make their own music."

The whole gathering exclaimed in surprise.

"Yes, they will have a complete crack at it. Any way they want to play, they can play. I will make them their own stage and their own place to perform. They will have a chance to play every variation of music they desire. Of course, they will have to create it all on their own. But they will be given a chance to show just how well their system works. I will give them every opportunity to prove that their music is better and their orchestration superior.

"In the process, you—all of you—will take notes, make comparisons between us and them. And in the end, I will let you make your own judgment—whether you want to stick with me or go to their side."

The group was silent. Then someone asked, "But will this just go on forever?"

The owner smiled. "No. There will be an end. I'll give everyone ample warning. But someday they—and you—will be called to account for what you have done with the things I gave you."

"A judgment, you mean?"

"Yes."

There was a vast silence. Then, "What happens now?"

"I'll explain it to them, and then we begin. The grand experiment, we'll call it. The final proof." There was another long pause. "My way. Or their way. You will each choose." The owner quietly looked into every pair of eyes.

"On with it, then," one of them said.

The owner grimaced. "It will not be easy work. They will still try to attack and hurt us."

"But why, sir? Why do they hate us so?"

The owner looked at them a long time. Finally, he shook his head. "Even I do not understand it. But it is part of what it means to be a musician, free, and under my care and in my kingdom. Everyone has a choice."

There was another long silence. Then the owner said, "There is much to do, much to learn, much to prove. Go to it. And we'll report every day about what we're seeing. Agreed?"

The shout went up uniformly, "Agreed!"

The grand experiment began.

3

The Man Who Wanted
to Take Over the World

There was once a man who wanted to take over the world.
He was not a big man. He was a little man. He was not a smart
man. He was rather simple. He was not a hard-working man.
He was usually lazy. Perhaps these were some clues to why he
wanted to take over the world.

But just the same—little, simple, and lazy—he had a big
ambition: he wanted to rule the world.

One day he sat down to plot out his strategy. "It has to be
simple," he said. "People do not understand complex things."
He scribbled on his little sheet of paper.

"It has to be bold," he commented, "for people prefer
the lightning stroke, the deft slash." He scribbled some more.

"It has to be complete," he said, "for nothing less than a
total takeover will do. People do not like picking up the
pieces." He continued scribbling.

He considered political, social, economic, and military
strategies. "Let's see now," he said, "how will I get myself into
power?"

The party in power had proved to be benevolent and
would not be voted out easily. The little man thought of trying
a coup d'état, but he didn't have the manpower or the nerve.
"If the party in power moves against me defensively, I'm dead
as dirt," he remarked and considered his other options.

"This is a democracy, so I might be voted in. But how?"
His little brain whizzed and zapped. But nothing came.

Then he hit upon the ultimate solution: "Promises," he said with exultation. "Promise them power, pleasure, things, happiness. That has always moved things before."

He considered the various kinds of promises he might make, ones that the party in power could never make. "First of all, complete liberty. I will promise to liberate them from the despotic rule of the Party. In that way I will capture their allegiance, for they will see me as their ticket to true freedom."

Next, he said, "I will offer them peace. And at no cost. By sticking with me and my plan, we will have world peace in only days. I will simply set up a central government that will oversee all operations. No conflicts will be possible." He paused. "Or allowed," he said triumphantly. "All will agree with me!"

He prided himself on his next promise. "Prosperity! Things will never be better. With central planning and perfect organization, everything will function like clockwork. Everyone will answer to me. With only one coordinator, we can't help but succeed."

But he knew he had to go further than this. He decided on a campaign against the Party. "We will portray all its faults in vivid detail. No one will mistake that the Party is a tyrant unworthy of respect and allegiance. The people themselves will rise up. The grass roots will have a voice. They will cast the deciding vote. I will be the organ of their desire. I will be their voice, their call, their cry in the night."

The little man stomped about his room quite puffed up with his own words. "I'm a poet, the spokesman for the oppressed, the help of the needy, the leader of the crestfallen. All will follow me to a glory greater than any yet imagined."

He then considered economic possibilities. He reviewed the capitalistic and communistic theories as well as all others in between in rapid succession. He saw strengths in each. "It will be an amalgamation of all that is good and a rejection of all that is bad," he said out loud. "All will work for themselves, but they will see that the common good is the good of all. All will work for me, for they will see that my good is their good. All will profit. All will have a humble piece of the pie. We'll divide everything equally." Of course, in the midst of that

31

statement it occurred to him, "Since I'm more equal than others, I'll get the biggest share."

Again, he smiled at his own words. "I am a genius," he said with a sigh.

"As for the military, there will be none. We will appeal to the heart, not the brawn. We will never force anyone, but we will sway them with bold words, appealing to the highest in mankind—his great desire for life, liberty, and the pursuit of happiness. We will abolish all tyranny. Ultimately, even I will fade into the background. I will go on to new worlds, and they will worship only my memory."

The little man stomped about his little room and scribbled furiously on his little pad. His sentences began to run together, and his words were barely legible. But beneath it all, he wrote, "Promise them everything. Give them everything. Demand everything."

Then he went out to survey the nation he planned to overtake.

It wasn't much, but it was a beginning. There were only two of them. A man, Adam, and a woman, Eve, his wife. He went after the woman first, saying to himself, "The way to a man's heart is through his wife."

He approached her and made his promises, deftly and persuasively. The woman was intrigued. She accepted everything he said. She cast her vote against the Party. Then she signed up her husband.

The little man smiled, "Now I am the man who rules the world."

But when he came by the next day to set up his office, he discovered that Adam had already set up his own office with a bronzed plaque on the desk. It read, "Adam: the man who rules the world."

The little man was enraged, but he decided he ought to see what the woman thought of this outrage before he did anything. When he found her, he saw that she had also fashioned a plaque. It was over the sink where she did the dishes, and it read, "Eve: the woman who rules the man who rules the world."

The little man was apoplectic. He stomped out into the sunshine and screamed at the Party that he had been tricked. The Party said nothing.

He could think of nothing but revenge. "How? How?" he cried as he paced about his little room. He scribbled and scribbled on his little pad with his little script and wrote late into the night.

The next morning he had it figured out. After the man and the woman had been driven from their home by the Party and began having children, the little man gave to each son a little plaque that read, "I am the man who rules the world." And to each daughter he gave a little plaque that read, "I am the woman who rules the man who rules the world."

The sons and daughters have been arguing and fighting and killing each other ever since about who has the original.

Meanwhile, the little man scribbles away into the night, devising his plans, dreaming his dreams, and ruling the people who rule the world.

4
Chess

Natas and the King sat down to the chessboard. They had played many such games. Each one was a master lesson in intrigue and trickery from Natas and flawless, sacrificial but wise action from the King.

The King always won. Sometimes a match went through many games with the King down one, two, or three games. But in the end, he always had a way of turning it around—even the apparently bad moves—for good. No one quite understood it. Never once had the King lost his most important piece, the queen. Now it was being said that Natas had learned a strategy that would take it.

The two players sat at the board: Natas, slit-eyed and crafty; the King, his palm open and plaintive. Then Natas spoke words no one expected. "We play to the death," he said. "One final game."

Natas had won many single games. It was the length of a match that always wore him down, that gave the King a chance to use his masterful wisdom. One game? Just one? How could the King agree?

Natas was shriveled and ugly, though once the handsomest in the realm. His constant intrigue, shrewd plots, and harrowing escapes had turned him into a brown, wrinkled bag of a man, plain and angry. Sour and sharp-tongued, he rarely lost a duel. But this was the King. He might see his final collapse.

"To the death," said Natas, his lip cruel and thin.

"If that is what you desire," replied the King, calmly returning Natas's gaze.

The host in the throne room recoiled with shock at Natas's challenge, but anyone who had long observed the growing conflict knew it had been coming to this.

"You are certain you want this?" asked the King. He seemed confident, yet anyone could tell he did not welcome the contest.

"Absolutely!" said Natas.

The King sighed. "All right, when do we begin?" Natas was a shrewd one. Mighty in word and thought. Crafty in plot. He was known to topple entire legions with a single sly piece of trickery.

"Today," said Natas, with a curl of his lip. "Today! And it will go to the end. To the death."

"You know the rules?" The King held up the Book. Its black cover glistened in the radiant light of the King's breastplate.

"I know your rules," Natas said contemptuously.

The rules. That was the means by which the King usually outfoxed the fox. Always there was something in them so clear and transparent that Natas missed it in his feverish determination to overthrow the King. No one violated them or could violate them. Even though Natas had tried to get around them many a time with lesser opponents, an appeal to the rules was enough to stop him from intrigue.

But Natas had a reputation. The feint. The fake. The sly trick. Many had tromped unknowingly into his traps and had fallen.

The King put the Book down on the table. "Then we will begin."

The board was set. King, queen, rook, bishop, knight, pawn. Arranged as usual. The master game of games. The duel of nerves and mind.

The host drew near as one and watched as the King sat at the table, taking the white. Natas always took black. "I like to see them make the first mistake—at the start," he said. "The rest is easy."

35

The King looked over his pieces. Natas waited. The King made the standard first step: king's pawn two spaces forward. Nothing dramatic.

Natas did the same.

Already a hush had fallen in the throne room. Opponents whispered bets. Allies of the King trembled and blanched as they watched.

Natas already had a third of the host on his side. Perhaps as the game moved along, more would retreat or even desert one side for another. This was unto death. The great sword hung on the wall above the Game Table.

The King moved again—the king's knight to king's bishop two. Nothing remarkable. Natas made a similar move, but it was the queen's knight to queen's bishop two.

It went back and forth. Natas claimed a pawn. The King took one also. Natas took a bishop. The King took a knight.

Then Natas laid a trap. It was a simple one. Every one of the host saw it immediately. Surely the King wouldn't trip on that one. A bishop, knight, queen combination. Three blows, and the King would lose a rook.

Then the King moved—right into the trap! There was no escape.

A cry went up in the gallery. What was he doing? The faithful stood aghast and terrified. They knew well what Natas would do with them, given the chance.

Natas smiled and rubbed his hands together. As he placed his queen, he snatched the rook from the board. He kissed it and threw it into the air, then whipped out his sword and flailed it over his head.

The rook shattered. "We don't play again, so why not destroy the pieces as they fall!" he shouted.

The King merely shook his head and made his next move. But he was down a rook now. It had been an important heist. How could it have been that simple?

Still, the King remained calm. He moved deftly, certainly. The play went on with little action. Feints. Attempts at traps. Escapes and defensive measures.

The host watched in horror. The King did not appear to be laying a trap. Rather, he appeared to be setting himself up to fall into one. In another move he would lose his second bishop and a knight. And claim nothing from Natas. What did he have in mind?

Natas sprang to his feet. His raspy glee reverberated through the hall. "There *is* no trick! The King has become senile!" He took the bishop and knight in two swift moves.

What was the King doing? Didn't he understand that this was unto death? He seemed to be stuck in a pattern. Nothing less than far superior wisdom could win now. How could the King avoid defeat? Even a youngster could win with odds like these.

Maybe it would have something to do with the rules. Years of intrigue and deception prevented Natas from seeing their power and truth, but the King knew them perfectly.

Natas stooped to make more moves. He sacrificed a bishop, a pawn. Then—he had the King cornered again. The King's forces appeared too weak to withstand the assault. Natas took the King's second rook and two pawns.

The host strained to see a bead of sweat, any sign of fear on the King's face. But he was impassive. Was he not afraid of losing all—his kingdom, his life?

The King made his move without a word. They exchanged pawns. Now the King was left with one knight, the queen, and several pawns. Natas still had both rooks, one bishop, his queen, and one pawn more than the King. The host was so quiet they could hear the King's breathing.

Natas moved.

The King moved.

Natas raised his hand and placed a piece, then clapped his hands together.

The King's queen was trapped. How could it have happened? The queen! Never before had he lost a queen. Never! If he lost the queen, all hope was gone. Natas would triumph. That was beyond certainty. It was carved in stone high as a mountain.

As Natas closed in, all froze.

He had her. The King's queen. Even the expense of a rook and the bishop was nothing.

The moment the rook took the square where the queen stood, Natas leaped up, snatching the queen away in his hand. He held it to his lips and kissed the little figurine. "The queen! I have won the queen! I have won! I have won!" He held it up for all to see, then in his wretched, clawlike hands he crushed the queen to bits of stone. What was left, he smashed under his heel and rubbed deep into the carpet.

He eyed the King. "Do you resign now?" He reached to grab the sword on the wall.

But the King shook his head. "The game is not yet over. Play on." He had a knight, his king, and three pawns. Natas still possessed a rook and his queen, as well as other minor pieces.

The room was dead quiet. The entire host fixed their eyes on the face of the King. He reached to the board and made a move. A pawn. Forward.

"A useless move!" cried Natas with a laugh. "It will never make the other side of the board!" He ignored the pawn, still several moves from the other side, and bored in on the King's king with his rook. He would have him in less than four moves.

The King moved the pawn again.

Natas set up his queen. His bishop would be next.

The King moved the king back one space.

Natas would be set up in one more move. Checkmate. Then death!

The King's hand poised over the board. Every eye fixed upon his fingers. What had he picked up? Not the pawn. Not the knight or the king. What had been there?

The gallery strained to see. Then he moved his piece. It would certainly be his last move. But his hand concealed the piece. He set it down and held it in place blocking Natas' final descent. The King had nothing that could have been moved there. He took his hand away.

The queen! The same queen Natas had crushed into the rug! How? It had cornered one of Natas's rooks, eliminating the possible checkmate.

The host gasped.

Natas roared. "What is this?"

The King said nothing.

Natas jumped up. "This is a cheat. There is no second queen. I have already destroyed the only one. And your pawn has not reached the other side of the board!"

The King picked up the Book of rules. "I asked you if you had read the rules before we began."

Natas ripped the Book out of the King's hand. "I have read the rules. What mischief is this?"

The King took the Book back from Natas and pointed to a section. Natas read. His face flared crimson as blood. "Unjust!" he shrieked. "Unfair! The King's queen cannot be restored after three moves never to be taken again! Impossible!"

"Those are the rules," the King said quietly.

"But it's not fair! How can anyone play such a game?" screamed Natas, his hair standing out on his neck, his lips blue, his eyes red and full of fire.

"You know the rules. Play on," said the King.

Natas sputtered, turned to the gallery, screamed obscenities. "This is not fair. I refuse."

The King stood up. "You posed the challenge. But if you want to desist, we will stop. All you must do is bow to me."

"Never!" screamed Natas. He looked at the board and was about to move. But he pushed himself back from the table. "If the King's queen can never be taken again," he said, banging his fist on the table, "then I can't win!"

The King set his jaw. "Who suggested you ever should, or could, win?"

Natas's eyes popped, and saliva drooled off his lip. "That's the way it is with games!" he screamed. "Everyone learns that in kindergarten. Each side has a fair chance at winning."

The King shook his head. "This isn't a game," he said quietly. "It is not played like a game. Not the way you have chosen to play it."

Natas leaned forward, his hands white on the edge of the playing table. "I can never win this contest. Is that correct?"

"That is correct," said the King.

Natas pulled his hair and looked to the gallery for help. But no one said a word. "Then why should I even play?" he screamed. "Why should I even challenge you if I can never win?"

The King gazed evenly at Natas for a moment. Then he turned to the board and took Natas's rook with his untakable queen. "Your move!"

Natas knocked over the players on the board and came around the table, whipping out his sword. "Answer me," he shrieked. "Why should I even play if I can't win?"

The King pushed the sword away from his chest. "You must answer that yourself, Natas. It is something I will never comprehend."

Natas lifted his hand and swiped across the King's neck with his sword. The sword shattered the moment it touched the King. The King turned to his guards. They grabbed Natas and held him.

"What am I supposed to do?" he screamed.

"Lay down your arms," said the King quietly. "Cease the rebellion. Change your mind. Give it up, come back, and do what you were called to do."

Natas seemed to be thinking, grasping at anything that might help him in that moment. "But what if I can win?"

"You can't."

Natas seethed, "How do I know you're telling me the truth?"

The King sighed and shook his head, pointing his finger at Natas. "You have to choose whether you believe me or not. But I am telling you the truth. You can never win, and if you continue in this, you will end up locked in the deepest dungeon of my kingdom where you will no longer have opportunity to influence and hurt others."

Natas shrieked a horrid, obscene shriek. "Then I'll kill you!" he screamed. "I'll kill you!"

The King was calm. "I repeat: you cannot do that. You will never do that."

Natas struggled, but the guards held him.

"Take him out," the King said with a hard swallow. "And all who are with him."

A huge entourage was taken out screaming and kicking. Once they were outside the palace, they stood hurling insults at the King who stood on the wall.

Suddenly, Natas rose up among them, having freed himself from the guards. "We'll take you!" he shouted. "We'll find a way."

"There is no way," the King said, undisturbed and turning away.

"Don't turn your back to me, scoundrel!" shouted Natas.

But the King went back to the throne room, where the chess board lay. The din outside gradually subsided. Soon it was reported that Natas had gone into the forest, presumably to make plans to attack.

"What will we do?" asked the King's general.

The King bowed his head and sighed. Slowly, he picked up the pieces on the table.

"Contain him," said the King. "We will not allow him to do further harm than is necessary."

"Will he ever turn back?" said the general.

"No," said the King. "His pride has taken too deep a root."

"Then why let him live?"

The King sighed. "For now it is necessary."

"But why?" The pain in the general's voice was evident.

The King fixed him with his eyes. "To insure that you yourself and the others do not also rebel."

The general was stunned. "I will never rebel, your Majesty."

"I know," said the King with a smile. He gently touched the general's shoulder with his hand. "Now I'd like to be alone."

The general went to the door and signaled to the others to leave. The King sat down and held the queen chess piece. For a long time he gripped it in his palm. When everyone was gone, the King closed his eyes and wept.

5
In Search of a Proper Mate

At first, I wasn't sure what he wanted. Princes don't often reveal their heart desires at the start of this kind of business.

Actually, I didn't even think he knew what he wanted. Of course, my opinion changed. I know now he had her pictured from the start, even before I got involved. He knew her before she was born. That's the kind of person the prince was. He could see her—every line, every curve, every movement of her soul. He knew her before her parents' parents were even a gleam of spirit light.

That's what mystified me about it all. Why he chose her became the raging question of my mind. I was almost afraid to ask him, though. She was so much less than he could have had.

But I'm getting ahead of things.

I'm a simple man. I do a job, and I try to do it well. But from the start I knew he didn't come for my advice, or even for me to make the match. He already had the match. He simply wanted it all down on paper, clearly drawn out. He likes things that way.

It wasn't really an investigation. Not like I usually make. He just wanted me to get all the details in front of him. "Lay it all out," he said. "So I can see it straight."

Understand, this was the most distressing, astonishing case of my career. If he weren't the prince, I would have told him no, I wouldn't be party to this, and been done with it. Actually, if it had been up to me, I'd have never brought her up in the first place. He wouldn't have ever known she existed.

But, of course, that was impossible.

So he wanted the facts? All right, that's what I'd give him. That would end it for sure. He certainly couldn't go through with it once he knew everything. She'd be a girl of the past.

How little I understood then.

Her name was Clesia. Not your typical name, I know. But, of course, he knew that beforehand too.

He came in on a Friday. I knew he wanted every important detail, so I figured it would take the whole weekend. I realized I'd have to be careful about it, how much I revealed and when. He was a hard case. Set on his course. If I were to retain any semblance of integrity and reputation, my work was cut out for me.

He came in the morning. Sure. Smiling. Ready for the miracle of his life. I couldn't believe it. Did he really think she was some kind of gem? Could he have thought so, knowing what she had done? Or was he just looking through a dozen fresh roses at a distance on a windy day?

I didn't know. But I wanted to be kind about it. I showed him the picture first. "It's a fair likeness," I said. "Very honest. No brush strokes or anything. Just straight, as you said you wanted it."

He smiled.

Then I showed him the photo. With you I'll be frank. If the picture was bad, the photo was wretched. She was, as they say in my business, a no-hoper. Pocked cheeks. Stringy hair. Makeup a mess. I'm no misogynist, and I try to be fair with every woman, but I'm telling you this honey was no bunny. She was, as my son says, "hurtin' for certain."

I don't mean to be colloquial, serious as this was. The photo could easily have sent men with strong stomachs to the latrine—immediately. And to think that he planned to marry the woman!

We got through the photo. He was pleased. He nodded his head and simply said, "This is Clesia."

I nodded, as though to confirm it, but he didn't sound disappointed. He said it with pride and a kind of leaping joy, the kind you feel deep in your heart so you want to jump.

I was nearly sick. But I pulled out the notebook and eyed him. "Are you sure you're ready for this?"

He nodded. "Of course. How could I not be? I have waited for this for many years."

He should have waited a lot longer, if you ask me. But I began the rundown on her—measurements, that stuff.

He just waved his hand and shook his head. "I already know that."

She had the figure of an eighty-year-old woman who had never had a figure to begin with. But he didn't even seem interested.

So I gave him the results of my personal interview. "Highly unintelligent. 'Dense,' as they say. Untrusting. Ceaseless complaints. Worried about everything. No interest in history. Reads little." I asked him if I should go on. It made me tired just to read the litany.

He nodded. "Read it all."

"Bad teeth. Poor eyesight. Poor housekeeper." I told him that every time I visited her, her house was in a state of such confusion and disgust that I had to interview her outside. Flies everywhere. The sink? Ugh! I wanted to retch on the spot. Did the woman know what soap was? Had she ever cleaned anything?

And her parents. The worst sort. Divorced. Her father a pimply man living with another woman. Her mother a nag and a witch. I mean a black magic, lotion potion, dead frogs and bat's wings witch, if you understand.

Still, you couldn't feel sorry for Clesia. She could have done something for herself. She wasn't totally helpless. I told him, "Manifestly lazy. Picks her teeth. Discourteous. Raucous. Abrasive voice. Likes to prance around in outlandish costumes and admire herself."

He asked me if I saw anything positive. It was then I began to think he really was looking for the worst possible case he could find. But he didn't seem like the type. He wasn't punishing himself, I was sure of it. You can tell in such cases by the way they talk. He just wasn't that type.

I was frank. "No. Not a shred of anything."

He just cleared his throat and looked away. "OK, go on."

I didn't want to break the really bad things to him if I could help it. I mean, he'd planned this, they said, for something like eternity. I didn't know precisely what that meant, but it had to be a long time. Still, he was forcing me to show him the worst. So I had to watch my step. Too much, and it might incite him, make him think I was completely against her.

I told him, "She's a gossip of the worst sort. Keeps no secrets. No confidences. Lives for learning about the dirt on everyone."

He didn't even blink. I knew the prince was a private man, so I thought that would throw him. But he didn't even clear his throat. He simply sat there.

So I went on. "It's my judgment that she's a very angry woman. Bitter. Resentful. Unforgiving. She's suspicious, extremely sensitive about every little thing. And jealous."

He laughed. I tell you, he laughed. I almost thought I had him. So I said, "I'm telling you, this woman is a major wretch."

He immediately fixed his eyes on me and gazed for what seemed a whole minute. I knew then that I'd overstepped my bounds. But he smiled and said, "Go on."

I felt apologetic. "Sorry. I'll try to keep my own opinion out of it." But I had nothing good to say about her. So I told him the first major thing I thought might give him pause.

"She's a slut."

I said it matter-of-factly. I didn't try to indicate whether I thought this was immoral or anything, though I knew very well what he thought on that score.

"I know she's not a virgin," he said.

"Not a virgin!" I cried. I couldn't hold it in. "Do you know what this woman does every chance she gets? She's lain around with every second guy in town," I said, hoping to see him blanch or something. "The doctor said she's a disease-carrying piece of vermin. He wouldn't touch her."

The prince didn't give a hint of pain or rejection. "She's committed adultery," I said, "though I don't know why any woman's husband would want her."

He waited, saying nothing.

"And she's accepted money for it. You know, prostitution."

Not a shadow of a doubt crossed his features. Was the man catatonic? Now I knew I had to start bringing out the really bad stuff. Ha! Bad stuff! As though I hadn't given him enough.

"She's a habitual liar. Can't trust a word she says. Uses drugs. Alcoholic. Several abortions." I thought that would get him, but he didn't flinch.

All right, he asked for it. "She is wanted for hundreds of crimes. Even now she awaits sentencing."

"What crimes?" he asked.

So there was life in him! Gladly would I tell him. "Perjury. Theft. Extortion. Blackmail. Sodomy. Perversion." I let it all come out in slow but staccatoed shots. I wanted it to sink in.

"Larceny. Embezzling. Cheating. Fraud."

Did I detect the slightest droop of his head?

"Picking pockets. Arson. Child molestation."

How any one person could do all this was beyond me. But of course, she was much more than your normal person.

"Loan-sharking. Idolatry. Witchcraft."

I let that last one out after a long pause. But I think the "droop" I'd spotted earlier was just a change of his position. He hadn't even sighed once. So I let him have it.

"Infanticide and murder."

"Is that all?" he asked.

Good heavens, was the man insane? "Is that all?" Didn't he know who he was? Or his father? I felt like strangling him. Wasn't this enough to push him away? I knew I'd have to really knock him. I said, "You realize that she's a slave."

"Yes."

"You'll have to buy her from her owner."

"I understand that." He didn't even blink.

All right, the big one. The really big one. "You realize you'll have to pay for all her crimes?"

46

A long pause. I almost found myself praying. At last there was a hint of integrity in him.

"Execution, you mean?"

I wanted to hit him hard. "Absolutely! No escape!"

He waited. He seemed to be thinking. I could hardly hold myself back. At last he was going to turn it over, leave this obsession.

"I'll have to die first?" he said. The same even voice.

"Absolutely. This woman is wanted in every country of our planet."

He cleared his throat again. "All right. I understand."

I slumped down in my seat. What was left? If that didn't put an end to it, what would?

There was one last thing: "She wants nothing to do with you. You do realize that, don't you?"

He laughed. *He laughed!* What did he think this was—"Challenging Situations"—the new TV game? Good grief! I was boiling. It made me sick to think he was not only considering this now but had been for years. He'd planned it. Plotted it. He would do it, regardless of what I said.

Then he said, "I guess that's to be expected, considering..."

"Yes," I said, as contemptuously as I could. "That is to be expected. And if I were you..."

He held up his hand. "Don't say it. I didn't come for your advice about what to do."

I threw the brief onto the table. I wanted to belt him in the face. Bring him to his senses. "So you're going to go through with it?"

He looked at me, amazed. Amazed! "Of course I am. It is written."

All right. I'd seen a lot of kooks, lamebrains, weirdos, and idiots in my life, but he made them all look like Marcus Aurelius, Aristotle, Socrates, and Virgil thrown together. Where was his reasoning? What on earth was he doing?

I had to ask him. "Why do you want her, Immanuel?" I addressed him by his name. I felt fatherly all of a sudden. Maybe I shouldn't have, but he didn't act as though I was out of line or anything.

47

He glanced around the room and finally fixed his gray eyes on me. He was such a handsome man. Godly. Earnest. Sincere. Every attribute—he had it. "I want her because it is my father's will that I take her," he said.

So Dad was the problem.

"But what does he see in her, for heaven's sake?" I cried, throwing up my hands.

He laughed. "Nothing." He said it so matter-of-factly that I almost fell over.

"Nothing!" I roared. "Nothing?"

He gazed at me as though he felt sorry for me. "Did you think my father or my brother or I saw something in her?"

I stammered and hemmed and hawed for a moment. It had never occurred to me, actually. "You see nothing in her? Nothing?" I said again, a bit more meekly.

"There is nothing in her that has made my father choose her," he said. "That's what I meant to say."

I had to agree. But . . .

"But why, then, have you chosen her to be the bride? Your father, that is. Why has he chosen her for you? You could have someone so much greater and more beautiful. Someone who could give you a reason for choosing her, at least."

He ran his fingers through his hair. "So you think there might be someone out there who merits the choice?"

I laughed. "Of course. There are many. I could give you five, ten, a hundred, a million better than Clesia. Right now. This very moment."

He shook his head. "You are looking at the surface of things, Levi. Every last one of them is as bad off as Clesia. Do you understand that?"

No, I didn't understand. What could he mean?

"Please understand," he said. "My father didn't choose Clesia because she is better than others. Or worse. Or ugly. Or beautiful. There is nothing in her or about her that caused my father to choose her."

I was curious. I really wanted to understand this. "So why did he choose her then? If there is nothing in her or about her, as you say, what caused the choice?"

"My father's sovereign right to choose," said the prince. So coolly. So plainly. "Because he is king."

I sat back in my seat and breathed deeply. I had to get this straight. "You mean to tell me that the only reason your father chose Clesia is because he has a right to do that, and he has exercised that right?"

The prince smiled and nodded like he was glad I understood. "Yes, I guess you could say it that way."

"All right," I said. I wanted to get a little deeper. "Then why didn't he choose any of the others? Why didn't he choose all of them? You could marry all of them if you wanted."

As I asked that question, I was frightened. Genuinely frightened. I don't even know why. But I thought I realized something about the king and the prince that I'd never seen before. I wasn't sure then what it was.

"You ask the key to a great mystery, Levi ben Jacob," the prince said. "If I answered your question, you would have to have a mind able to comprehend the mind of my father himself."

"But is it fair?" I shouted. "Choosing Clesia but all these others just left aside?" Now I felt angry and upset.

He looked down and grimaced. "You ask a hard question. But let me answer it this way. Is there anything in Clesia or any of the others that requires that I choose them—I, the prince, or my father, the king?"

I thought about that. I really thought about it. But I didn't have to think long. I knew the answer. I spoke quietly, much more subdued. "No, I suppose there is nothing that requires you to choose them. Otherwise, it's no longer your choice, but theirs. Or some higher rule making you do the choosing, which makes the rule greater than the king."

He said, "You are a wise man, Levi. But you have much to learn. We must make preparations for the wedding. But first, the hard part."

"The hard part?" I didn't know what he was referring to.

"Yes," he said. "You did say she had committed crimes worthy of death?"

"Yes."

For the first time, he blanched. He closed his eyes, and I could see pain jolt through him. I reached out to grab him, but he held up his hand. "I'm all right," he said. "It's just that even now I'm not sure how great the cost will be. But if I am to marry Clesia, I must pay it, mustn't I?"

It was almost as though he were hoping I would tell him there was some way around all that. But I knew there wasn't. And so did he. He got up and turned to go. Then he turned around and held out his hand. "You have done a good job, Levi. I am grateful. Perhaps what you have done will help her understand. Do you think so?"

I looked at her picture lying on the table. It was a stifling feeling. What he had to do. What he was going to do.

And her. The kind of woman she was. Would she ever understand what he would do for her, what price he had to pay to make her his bride? Could she? Ever?

Middles

6
Out of the River

I can't remember quite how I got into the river, though I recall it was pleasant. The river rolled along, pitching us here and there, eddying and playing, spraying our faces. We had plenty of time for talk and cards and whatnot. No one had any particularly enchanting explanation for how it all started. Of course, there were speculations.

Some said we'd been here all along; it never ended; the river just went on and on. Others said we were part of it; we'd grown up and changed with it. Still others claimed that there was no need to question; just enjoy. And then there were those who said it hadn't always been like this, but some ancestral sin had put us into it.

Just the same, it didn't seem so bad if you were one of the rich ones, or had everything taken care of.

Then the rescuer arrived. He was this burly, friendly fellow. He didn't talk much. But suddenly he was there in the river next to me. I had been sipping some River-ade, watching one of our troupes put on a water polo exhibition. When I turned my head, he was there.

"I've come to rescue you," he said. He began to put his arm over my chest.

"Wait," I cried. "Rescue me from what? I didn't know I needed rescuing."

He said quietly, "The river is running toward a waterfall. You'll be dashed on the rocks."

I laughed. "I've heard about the waterfall. Many say it's not true."

"It's true."

Something about the way he talked rang fear through my bones. But I countered, "How do I know it's true?"

"There is no need of proof except that I say it's true."

I snickered. "And who are you to go about telling everyone you know the truth?"

"I'm the rescuer," he said. "Whatever I say is by its nature true. I can speak nothing but truth. You can rely on me for that. And I assure you, you are headed for the waterfall."

"What if I don't go along with this?" I asked. "What if I refuse?"

He replied, "That's your choice. I will take whatever action I choose in such an event."

It was a startling answer. Nothing threw him. He stayed calm.

"Where will you take me?" I asked.

"To safety."

"Where is that?"

"I'll show you."

I laughed again. "You speak in circles. This doesn't make any sense."

"It will," he said.

I shook my head, smiling. "You're the strangest person I've ever met."

This time he chuckled. "Many say that. But I've come to rescue you. Are you ready?"

I gulped. "You're being rather pushy about this."

He said, "I won't force you. Would you rather I left you alone?"

"But what if I decided I wanted rescue later?"

"I might not be available later."

I gulped again. I searched his eyes to see if this wasn't some new lie. I'd seen a lot of lies in the river. You learned to trust no one, not even yourself. But I could detect no falsehood.

"OK," I said. "Take me."

He put his arm over my chest and began pulling me toward the bank of the river. I'd seen the land often enough before. A desolate place. No one but fools went there. No one quite understood how to get there, but everyone was sure there was no reason to leave the river. It was cold and damp and appeared to be lifeless.

The rescuer set me upon the shore. "Make yourself at home and move inland. Whenever you want to talk, call me. I'll come. If you need anything, just ask. Only keep moving inland. Also, think of any you know in the river that you want me to rescue. I'll be asking you frequently for names."

He paused. Then he said with grave precision, "Whatever you do, don't go back into the river, no matter what anyone says. I don't make it a habit to pull out people twice." I watched as he dove back into the river. Already he was speaking with another.

The ground was hard. The air was cold. I saw others wandering around on the shore. Some seemed lost. Several were making their way inland.

I turned back toward the river, and suddenly I was struck with the most incredible longing.

"Just a quick dive," said a voice. "You'll be warm again." But I remembered the rescuer's words and hesitated.

The voice said again, "How do you know he's right? A quick dive can't hurt."

"But he said," I protested, "I shouldn't do it."

"Why not?" said the voice. "What harm can there be?"

I thought about it. I didn't know. But something within me had changed. I liked the solid feel of the ground. Not a whole lot. It hurt my feet. Yet it gave one a contented feeling. Not like the river—always changing, never clear about what was coming next.

I watched the rescuer. He was pulling people out all over the river. He worked quickly. Twice I saw him strike a man in the jaw and knock him out to get him out of the river. On another occasion, I watched him argue for nearly an hour. That man also succumbed. But there were others. Some he approached and after only a brief conversation, left. I never saw him rescue them. He argued with one for several hours, then stopped abruptly. He left that one swirling along alone. He talked to two of them several times, went and rescued others in between, and then came back to them. One, he finally did rescue. The other, I don't know.

The amazing thing was that he approached everyone at least once, and many were approached often. I couldn't see how he kept it up, but he did.

As he rescued more and more people, a small group gathered around me. We began to talk. "Isn't it wonderful?" said one. "He rescued all of us from the waterfall."

"Yeah, but how do we know there's really a waterfall?" asked another.

No one had an answer. But someone said, "I guess we just have to believe him."

Most agreed. But one was angry. "I think it's wrong that he barged into my quiet existence and demanded to rescue me. I'm going back into the river." Several tried to stop him, but he dove in. We didn't see him again.

We began walking inland together. One turned back and watched the rescuer for a while. When he caught up to us, he was angry. "He didn't rescue Uncle Pete."

Soon the whole group was in a state of upset.

"Yeah, and my father went down toward the waterfall, too," another said. "I only saw the rescuer talk to him once."

A third remembered a sister who hadn't been rescued. It seemed everyone knew someone he didn't rescue. "He's a bit unfair about this," said one, "rescuing some and letting others go."

I replied, "But he approached them all."

"He could've fought with them," answered another.

"That's what he did to me. I'm glad that he did. Why didn't he do that to others if they wouldn't go along with him?"

We had no answers.

"Perhaps we ought to ask him. That's what he told me to do," I said.

"Right," answered another. "Let's ask him."

We all began shouting our question, and instantly, the rescuer was among us. Each brought his protest. "Why didn't you rescue my mother?" "What about my sister, Jo?" "How come you didn't knock out my cousin, Anthony?" And, "Why did you only talk once to my partner, Bill?"

The rescuer was silent for a long time. We all waited, somewhat impatiently. Finally, he said, "I choose to rescue whom I will rescue. I choose when to start and when to complete a rescue and when to leave it off. That is my choice because I'm the rescuer."

"But what did they do," cried another, "to make you leave them?"

"Many things," said the rescuer. "Some argued, some fought, some dove back in. There are many reasons I choose not to rescue a person."

"Then what did we do that made you rescue us?" asked still another.

The rescuer smiled. "Nothing."

The group exploded with anger. "Nothing!" shouted one. "You rescued us for no reason?"

"Not 'no reason,'" said the rescuer. "I rescued you for reasons known only to myself. But, I assure you, it had nothing to do with anything about you, or in you, or that you did. I chose to rescue you because I love you."

Everyone was silent.

But then a lady voiced the question that was on all our hearts. "But why do you love us? There must be some reason."

"Because I'm love itself," said the rescuer.

"You mean there was nothing in us or about us that made you love us?" said the woman, miffed and unhappy.

"Nothing."

We were all frightened and worried about this. But the rescuer said, "Think of it this way. My love and choice of you is not dependent on anything about you or in you. It's totally dependent on me. That should give you great security."

Frankly, I didn't know what to think. But it did make sense. In fact, the more I thought about it, the more settled I felt. Finally, I said, "If this is so, then we have every reason to love you all the more."

The rescuer said nothing.

Another member of the group said, "But why don't you rescue all of them?"

The rescuer was quiet again. Then he said, "That is not how I've chosen to do it."

"But why?" said another. "Why don't you choose to do it another way?"

The rescuer peered into our faces. He said, "Don't you do as you please with what is yours? I do as I please with what is mine."

I said, "You mean you own us, the river, everything?"

"Yes."

Everyone was upset again. Then a small voice—a child—spoke up from the back. "Why did you rescue me?"

We turned and looked at the little boy. He was deformed, ugly. He couldn't even walk upright. No one had noticed him before.

The rescuer's eyes were tender. "Because I love you."

"As much as everyone else?" said the lad, a tear forming in his eye. It was obvious he'd known much pain in the river.

"I love everyone equally," said the rescuer, "but I also love them infinitely. I love you infinitely also. There is no end to my love for you."

Some members of the group were weeping now. My own throat was feeling taut, but I managed to say, "What if you hadn't rescued us?"

"You would have gone over the waterfall."

"Isn't there some other way?" another said.

"None," he said. He didn't say this as if it were an unhappy state of affairs or he wished it were otherwise. He just said it.

"If you didn't rescue us, wouldn't someone else?"

"There is no one else," he said quietly.

I gulped. "But if there's nothing about us that makes us worthy, it is amazing that you rescue anyone."

The rescuer gazed steadily at us, saying nothing.

"How did we get into the river?" asked a man in the back with a beard. "It seems that the whole problem is our being in the river."

The rescuer looked him firmly in the eye. "You put your-self in the river," he said.

We all gasped. I'd heard it before, but I never really be-lieved it. The man said, "When? I don't remember that."

"After the beginning."

"You mean we weren't always in the river?"

"No." He let this sink in and seemed about to turn to go, but a large man jumped up and gestured a moment. "Can I say something?" he asked.

The rescuer nodded.

"If we put ourselves into the river, couldn't get out on our own, and would have gone over the waterfall if you hadn't done something, then you have done us a great service." Ev-eryone agreed.

"Then," said the man, "although I don't have much, I want to offer you my life for service and worship. Will you take it?"

The rescuer gazed steadily at all of us. It seemed, as he caught my eye, that he looked through me, into the depths of my soul. I quivered and suddenly felt afraid in his presence. Almost without thinking, I knelt before him and said, "You are my lord. I'll follow you wherever you go."

I can't quite explain it, but that moment was astounding. He didn't act as though we had done him a great service, nor did he appear to regard our deeds as worthless. It was as though he saw that this was as it should be. He enjoyed it, and he desired it without demanding it.

Suddenly, he cried, "To the uplands! Move inward and upward. Run! You must learn more."

We all began to move. Some ran, some walked, some la-bored, limping and tired. But all of us moved onward, helping one another, encouraging one another. Few ever looked back to the river with longing.

7
The Hedge

This report was discovered in the recent archaeological find, now known as "The Lucifer Papers." It appears to be a report turned in by a member of the Sixth Quadrant, Eighth Deceivaliers. His name was actually Hoo-ku-la-na-zee-ah, but his fellow demons called him "Tug," and this is the name he uses in the report.

He could not have been of higher rank than a Principality Sixth, which means he was in charge of a Tempt Team. However, he was obviously given a leave of absence to provide this important study on "the hedge" (a term taken from Lucifer's complaint to God in Job 1:10 to describe a protection God puts around believers against the onslaughts of the forces of darkness).

It appears also that this report provided resource material he used later to win an honorary mention in the annual essay contest sponsored by *Accuser Monthly,* a much read rag among the residents of the Pit.

Report

Day 1: I arrived on the site this morning and took several readings on the hedge before settling into my quarters under a rock on a hill not far from the house. My subject is known as Joseph Saunders, converted to faith in Christ about the age of twelve. He apparently has little knowledge of the hedge as he complains frequently to the Enemy about his lack of success in sports and his frequent Bs and Cs on tests.

When I approached, the hedge intensified instantly, but I was able to lob a few thought-bombs over it and send J. S. into a brief spate of discouragement. However, I was not able to afflict him with anything physical, nor could I attack his dog or his cat (but they both smelled so bad, I didn't make much of an effort).

Day 2: Clearly, the hedge is not a form of vegetation or other material. It appears to be fabricated of some kind of light. Undoubtedly, it is divine light that Saunders can't see at all but which is constantly apparent to me. I wonder why light of this sort is so repulsive to us now that we have been cast out of heaven. We used to bask in it all the time.

Just the same, I could not penetrate it.

Day 3: Tried the following weapons on the hedge to no effect:
Incantations.
Lucifer's name.
Shouting.
A clod of dirt. (It fell at his feet, and he picked it up, laughed, then threw it at the barn, saying, "I bet I could outpitch Tug McGraw," which I thought at first was some indication that he knew about me. Later, I learned that he was referring to some pitcher in the American Baseball League. Saunders is quite a fan, and I learned a lot about ERAs, batting averages, and umpires.)
His mother. (I tried to incite her against him by reminding her that he'd left his socks on the floor again.)
A stray dog.
Two other demons. (Boo-zzzzooo-li-nu-no and Ippa-ippa-ippa-oo, both of whom, as you know, are ranked far below me and were not endowed with much intelligence to begin with, but I thought their stupidity would aid them since the hedge's light can singe us. However, they were both burned and vowed to "get me back" in another eon or two. I didn't take their threat as much, since I know their ranking demon.)

A rock album. (It did hurt his ears, but he didn't seem to know.)

The only things that did get through were accusations (I told Saunders he was a lousy son, and he went in, lay down on the bed, and stared at the wall for a while), diversions (I reminded him when he got up to read his Bible that he really ought to have a glass of milk, which he did, and promptly forgot about reading the Bible), and incitements (I suggested that his girlfriend was making too many demands, and he engaged her in an argument about the merits of McDonald's over Burger King).

Day 4: Not much action today. Saunders has been taking some courses in zoology—he thinks he might like to be a botanist of all things—and I became rather irritated with his complaints about weevils. He kept calling them "stupid little devils," and frankly, I took offense. What gives these humans the right to compare us—the majestic rulers of the universe—to bugs and weevils? I hear these kinds of things all the time from these bipeds, and it makes me wild. Just wait till I can get at this fellow.

Anyway, I did a little reading in Con's *Close Encounters with the Hedge*. One interesting comment he made was this: "You can sometimes appeal (or send one of our lawyers to appeal) to the Enemy for the right to penetrate the hedge and be given free rein over your charge. We've done this on other occasions (Job, Peter). Generally, our contention is that given the chance we will prove once and for all that a man is not truly allied in his heart to the Enemy. Most believers initially find it simple to 'trust in the Lord' and make gigantic verbal confessions. (And the Enemy is such a sentimental prig that He receives those confessions, even before the supplicant changes his behavior.) But when we put them through the fire, we often find that what was expressed in words goes up in the smoke."

He added this anecdote:

"I know of one young man who went along for many years as a church member, then as leader of his youth group, and finally as a helper in a Sunday school class. He gave testimonies of his dramatic conversion—how he came to you-know-who at some evangelistic campaign, studied the Bible, gave liberally of what he earned cutting people's lawns, and kept his life clean. He was what many call a 'model Christian.'

"But our lawyers petitioned repeatedly for a chance to try him, and the Enemy finally relented. We rammed the saint's girlfriend into a truck as she drove to church, and the girl lost a leg. The lad was incensed. He was one of those types that believed nothing bad ever happens to real Christians. Next, we smote him with some horrid tooth problems. And last of all, we led his best friend into a cult. The boy turned bitter, cursed God to His face, and lived a godless (but clean) life thereafter. The beauty of it was that he didn't leap off into sin or even quit going to church. That was too ingrained in him. But in his heart, he hated and resented the Enemy. Eventually he drifted away when he moved to another city and died an embittered hater of God. He's safely entombed below."

It appears to me that this petitioning process ought to be stepped up at all costs.

Day 5: Received word that our lawyers are petitioning the Enemy even now for an occasion for me against Saunders. I'd like to give Saunders a thunderbolt or a good whack of acne. (The wretch has a clear complexion, and I haven't been able to slay him with "self-image" problems as much of late.) Just yesterday he made a snide comment to his mother that he thought the devil was giving him a hard time, but he knew God was with him, and he'd asked the Enemy to rebuke me.

Imagine!

Am planning to listen to a tape by Riddleslick, one of my favorite speakers. The tape is titled "Up with an Insult, Down with the Hedge." Something about our petitioning process. I think he says that if you can't harass the Enemy into letting down the hedge, you can certainly insult Him into it. Should be interesting.

I am finding that if I can enlist his girlfriend to wear some of that lacy "see through" clothing, it gets him so bothered that his mind stays far away from spiritual things. She's a most "spiritual"—perish the word—young lady, as you know, and prays every day. But she has no idea what her sexy dress does to this young man. If I can get her to wear one low-slung blouse, his mind is undressing her completely in only seconds. Such an aside can sidetrack him for weeks and keep him in a state of arousement every time he's near her. (Is that the right word? We don't seem to understand this human capability very well.) I've even had success in getting him to try to persuade her to do other things besides kiss, virtually frying the lad for the evening. (Her motto is Everything Above the Neck Is All Right. Quaint, but it will have to be dislodged; I'll see if I can get her demon working on it.)

But what's all this have to do with the hedge? I still haven't been able to penetrate it with anything close to a good boil, pimple, allergy, or shot to the jaw. I can't even seem to incite any of the local wiseacres who call him a "nerd" to give him a hard time in his classes. (*Nerd*—interesting word. Do they realize that in Egyptian it means "one who will eventually rule you"? I don't think so.)

Day 6: Have been listening to Riddleslick quite excitedly. He suggests that there is a weak point in every hedge somewhere. Of course, that's the main reason I'm on this expedition, to find such a point—a slot I can seep through, or some crack or hole I can shoot through—something. Riddleslick says, "Don't tell me there is no weak point. As much as the Enemy makes of His powers, we know that He's not invincible. So keep looking for that single crack through which you can tear and shear off a man's faith."

He also promises that our lawyers are always working to gain us such opportunities, and therefore we must be thinking ahead about what we'll do. I know very well what I'll do to Saunders if I get a chance: hail in one of those motorcycle gangs to rough him up and get him to deny the faith. It's simple. I know two fellows I could bring in with only the promise of beer and pretzels for all.

Day 7: Been looking hard for the "crack" in the hedge. In the process, I discovered the power of suggestion can sometimes work the wrong way. For instance, today Saunders was a bit angry with his girl and wanted to scare her. I suggested he take his dad's 1983 Thunderbird and make some thunder of his own. He'd never done anything quite like it before. His girlfriend said that she wanted to get out of the car, but he just pushed the "pedal to the metal" (That's what he called it. I'm not quite sure what it means, but I like the rhyme.) and gave her a whirl. She said he was sinning and deserved to have the Lord discipline him. (This girl has quite a mouth, I tell you, but I've found most women speak their minds to men if they feel secure in their love.) I hit him with, "Why don't you see if the Lord really will protect you? Take it up to ninety."

It was terrible. He pushed that car up to eighty-five, his girl was screaming. I watched what was going on in his mind, and the terrible part was that you-know-who was talking almost directly to him, telling him he was tempting the Lord. He began to sweat and pulled back immediately. I realized then that I have to be careful that the Enemy doesn't come up with some counterattack that ruins my best efforts.

Day 16: I think I've found the hole in the hedge. It will open only at certain moments, but if you catch it right, I'm confident you can get in and devour the subject in seconds. Here's my plan.

You know how they're always saying the Enemy never sleeps, is always watching, never deserts His own, and so on and so forth? Well, Saunders was watching a movie, and they did a little trick in it. A couple of soldiers were being followed by an enemy soldier who had a weapon. In order to put him off guard, they threw a stone to their left. When it clunked to the ground, the enemy soldier shifted in that direction. And presto, the two others jumped him.

This is my ploy: I think that if I can divert the Enemy from His watchfulness—perhaps by some sort of verbal "stone"—the hedge will open up, and I'll be in.

But if that doesn't work, I have something else. I'm confident that if I can get Saunders to sin in some way, the Enemy will blink His eyes in sheer horror, and my chance will be at hand. What do you think?

65

Day 20: Well, I've discovered the Enemy can be neither diverted nor put to sleep. And His eyes don't blink. What to do now?

Day 31: Our lawyers informed me that the Enemy has relented. He has given me an occasion against Saunders. The hedge will be down tomorrow for two days. I can do anything I want to him—well, not quite anything, but at least I can smite him with depression and anxiety. That may be enough.

Day 32: This is unimaginable. Frankly, I don't know what happened. I'm in a jungle somewhere, and there's nothing here but macaws and monkeys. The smell is terrible.

Last thing I remember was catching Saunders in a blue funk about his spiritual life, sneaking up to the hedge, looking for the chink, getting ready to slide through, and suddenly this voice out of heaven rapped right into me—making my horns crinkle up. "Get thee to . . . " some place I didn't recognize.

Suddenly, I found myself here. What gives?

Day 46: An awful session with my superior. He told me the Enemy informed our lawyers there was no touching Saunders or lifting the hedge. Apparently, they lied to me hoping to get me to try something radical. And at my expense! The Enemy wouldn't listen to any of our insults or threats after that. That was when I was zapped. There was no time to warn me, they said, as there was a big persecution going on in China; so many were being converted that for months tempters had been pulling triple and quadruple shifts without a break.

Day 48: A new assignment—finding ways to catch a prayer on its way to heaven, decode it, and then jam the signal. Won't be messing with hedges for a while.

Memo

TO: Tug
FR: Doss

Your lack of success with the hedge is understandable. But we're sure of breakthroughs any day now. You're not the only one on such studies, though we've had trouble retrieving several tempters of late. We even found one floating about on an iceberg. The poor demon was so frozen over that we had to cast him into hell just to warm his tongue.

Let me offer a word of counsel, though. Don't give up on penetrating that hedge. There is a way. Lucifer knows it. Remember, this is no game we're playing. This is war. We don't attack these bipeds simply to irk the Enemy. In fact, Lucifer is putting together a gallery for exhibition just in case we ever have to answer for anything. I've brought a few of my rankest charges down into hell just for that purpose. If there's ever a reason to make comparisons—my deeds to theirs—I'm quite sure these infidels will far outstrip me in wickedness. This way we can make a defense. The Enemy does make much of these little insubordinations and disagreements, saying we'll all burn forever, and so on and so forth. He never lets a sin get by without just recompense. And except for that abomination on Calvary, there's no way around it.

Remember what He did to David for his crimes with Bathsheba? Even with the man's repentance, there were still consequences for the sin. For that reason, I regard some of these quacks we've confined in hell as fire insurance. You'd do well to provide the same.

Good luck on that prayer jamming mission.

8
Answers

There was once a young man named Harry who possessed most of the good things life can offer: a brand-name stereo; a hard, flat bed that kept his back straight and supple; kind professors who gave him fair grades and a day off now and then; and a sister who didn't bug him too much about which girls he liked.

But for some reason, he was dissatisfied. Certain questions kept creeping into his consciousness. Questions like, "What happens when you die?" and, "Is there a purpose for my existence?" and, "What should I do with my life?" In particular it had come to his attention that life wasn't all it was cracked up to be, which raised the question, "What exactly *was* it cracked up to be?" He decided to ask his mother. He said, "Mother, I've got some questions about life. Can you help me?"

She sat down, pushed her glasses onto the end of her nose, and said nervously, "OK, what are they?"

Harry asked her about death, the purpose of life, why he was born, things like that. She wasn't pleased and shook her head. "What do you think I am, Harry, a philosopher? Go ask your father."

So he approached his father while he was working in the basement fixing a lamp. "Dad," he said, "can you tell me what life is all about?"

His father laughed. "You tell me. I been trying to figure that one out ever since I married your mother."

Harry was serious though and pressed on. "No, I really want to know. What happens when you die?"

His father looked down at the floor for a moment, then said, "That's what I'm sending you to college for. When you find out, let me know."

Harry felt a bit frustrated, but he didn't mention it again to him. When he got to college, he began asking the same questions of his professors. His math prof said, "A philosophy major. That's what you ought to be. Sign up for Phil. 101, son. It'll straighten you out."

He signed up for Phil. 101. But instead of answering his questions, it only raised more questions. And when he began demanding answers, they told him, "Look, if you want concrete answers, become a scientist. We're mainly into questions."

He decided to major in mechanical engineering. He had to admit it was simpler. After graduation, he took his first job. Building motors, checking tolerances, and arranging superstructures gave him a lot of concrete to play with.

But he still felt vaguely dissatisfied. It wasn't that he couldn't enjoy things. Not at all. His friends saw him as a generally happy-go-lucky guy. He was reaching for the stars, and for the most part he was grabbing them. His work partners thought him a little weird and even dubbed him the office sage, but he didn't mind and kept asking his questions. He didn't talk a lot about his sense of dissatisfaction, though. When he did, people seemed hurt, as though he had insulted them personally. When he mentioned it to an associate, his friend only said, "Maybe you're a victim of burnout. Have you seen a doctor lately?"

He made an appointment the next week. But after a physical and a friendly chat, the doctor only said, "I can understand how you feel, but I think you simply need to find a wife and raise a family. That'll give you plenty of meaning and not much time for sitting around worrying about what happens after death."

So he got married, had two children, bought a house, kept the fireplace clean, took out the trash, and gave his wife a fair allowance. The food was good. He had lots of relaxation (except around income tax time), and the vacations were excellent. He took loads of pictures and showed them to his friends. He had no complaints about his home, money, boss, or how his wife folded his socks, though of course he recognized everyone had room for improvement. He learned to be assertive, to pull his own strings, to jog and play racquetball, and to spend time with his family. He didn't even watch much television or waste his time with cheap novels. He was respected and loved. But he remained dissatisfied. "There's something missing," he told himself. "But what?"

He sat down with a friend one day and told him how he felt. His friend was sympathetic but didn't understand. "If you're not happy, who is? Why, I already think of you as the happiest person I know. Don't worry about all this stuff. It'll work out."

But it didn't. His insides were squeezing out. He went to see his pastor.

Harry took a seat in the overstuffed chair in the office. The pastor folded his hands over his desk and asked, "What can I do for you?"

Harry said, "I don't know, Reverend. It just seems that I've got all these questions floating around. I want to know why I'm here, where I'm going, if there's a God, and what happens when you die. Is that so hard?"

The reverend smiled. "Men have been asking those questions since time began."

"OK, so what have we found out?"

"Well, if you look at Christianity you see one answer, and if you look at Buddhism, there's another. And if you look at Judaism, there's a third. You have to decide for yourself. I'd be willing to give you some books."

Harry took the books home and read for hours. Like the pastor had said, everyone seemed to have his own little theory. Most of the theories excluded one another too, so the turmoil in his mind only grew. "Why can't anyone answer a few simple questions?" he shouted in his rec room one day. But his wife only shook her head and continued to stir a pot of pinto beans and franks.

70

One day at work a friend edged into his office and said, "Harry, I want to tell you something."

Harry looked up.

His friend said, "Harry, I've found God. It's the most exciting thing that ever happened to me."

"What?" said Harry and jumped up.

"Yeah," he said. "I've been born again."

"What's that?"

"It's like starting over, only better. For the first time in my life I feel at peace."

"What happened?"

His friend breathed deeply and scratched his nose. "Well, I don't really know. I've been going to this Bible study and learning about Jesus, and one day it all seemed to come together in my head. So I decided I wanted to follow Him and accept His forgiveness."

Harry had to admit he was interested but skeptical. "How do you know it's for real?"

His friend shook his head. "I guess in a way, I don't. But it feels real, like He's there with you everywhere you go."

"It's not a psychological trip?"

"I don't think so. I'm a pretty down-to-earth guy."

"But what if it wears off? How can you be sure it'll last?"

"It's strange," he said. "It feels different—like it lasts forever."

"So how do I get to meet this God of yours?"

His friend became excited. "Just trust Jesus. Call on Him, and He'll save you. That's all there is to it."

"Just trust Jesus," said Harry, feeling the air go out of him. "I hardly know who Jesus is. How can I trust Him? I have enough trouble trusting my lawyer."

His friend screwed up his face and sighed. "I don't know what to say. I guess I thought I'd just tell you what happened, and you'd want it too."

"OK," Harry said. "What do I do?"

His friend looked nervous, then said, "Just pray, I guess."

Harry prayed. When he was done, he said, "Well?"

His friend was looking at him strangely. "Anything happen?"

Harry shrugged. "Nothing I can see."

His friend shook his head. "I don't know. I don't know. I guess you don't have enough faith or something."

Harry sat down in his chair and exhaled. When his friend walked out of the office, he felt a deep darkness falling over his soul. "I've tried everything," he murmured. "And I haven't found the answers. I guess there are none."

The darkness only grew. By the time he left work, Harry was so despondent that he wanted to die. On the way home, he flew into a rage at God. "If you're there, why are you making it so difficult? Where are you? Who are you? If you're there, I demand an answer."

Harry listened intently, half expecting the roof of the car to split open. But there was no sound except a horn blaring as Harry drifted into another lane. His heart jolted, and he swerved back into his right lane. "That was close," he mumbled.

But he found himself praying again. "All right, God, I've tried everything. I've read books, asked everybody questions, and no one seems to have the answers. What should I do?"

Again, he listened intently. But he only heard his own heart beating.

Then an idea hit him. "OK, God, we'll do this. You do it your way. I'll just go along as things are and expect that you're going to help me find you. I leave it in your hands."

It seemed logical to Harry, so he didn't think about it for the rest of the ride home. He was even whistling when he walked in the door and greeted his wife. That night he played with the children, watched a little television, and read the paper. In the back of his mind was a quietness that hadn't been there before, but he didn't think about it.

Before bed though, he noticed a Bible on his wife's bedstand. "Mind if I read it for a little while?" he asked her.

"Go ahead," she said with a smile.

Harry didn't know where to start, but he opened to Luke and read the first few chapters.

Over the next few weeks, he read Luke, Romans (which he didn't understand at all), Revelation (he gave up at the seventh chapter), then Mark, and finally John. Slowly, ideas were forming in his mind.

And one night, as he was reading the last few chapters of John, it hit him. "Jesus was God!" he exclaimed out loud.

His wife jumped and stared at him. But then she patted his hand. "I've been praying that you'd get that for a long time."

"It's true," he said. "I know it."

"How?" she asked.

He thought about it. "Well, I've been reading the Bible, and I prayed, and of course we've gone to church."

But there was something more, something deeper. He tried to think of what it was. Then he had it. "God Himself showed me. He's opened my eyes. Like I prayed months ago!"

He put his arm on his wife's shoulder and lay back. "All that time asking questions, and it was so simple—I should have been asking God all along."

"Well, why don't you tell Him thanks?"

He nodded. "I think that's just what I'll do." And he bowed his head and began to pray.

But this time he knew to whom he was praying.

9
Gepetto's Toy Shop

There was a toy-maker named Gepetto who was known as the greatest toy-maker ever. His toys had greater beauty, character, and abilities than any others ever invented. They talked. They walked. They even made their own decisions in the toy shop. If one preferred this shelf to another, he simply had to climb up there and make himself at home. If one wanted to wave a stick and shout "Rah," all he had to do was do it.

Of course, this created problems. Occasionally two toys wanted the same spot. There were also many disputes about sticks and whatnot. In fact, most of the toys spent more time arguing than anything else.

Then one of the toys named Hoolie discovered a long letter from Gepetto. The dust on it was thick, for it had lain on a shelf for years. But when Hoolie read it, the words were as alive as though they'd been written yesterday. He began telling everyone about it. "The letter talks all about Gepetto and how he originally made us," he told the gorilla, giraffe, and black bear.

Hoolie told the toy trains and the autocars, "He tells us how to settle disputes and how to get along with one another."

To the lion he said, "Gepetto even says we can become much more than toys—we can become just like him in character, perfect and free." Many began reading the letter, and soon they were all discussing it.

74

"How do we know this letter is really from Gepetto?" asked the lion. "One of the other toys here could have made it up."

"Who?" asked Hoolie.

No one knew.

"It came from long ago," said the hippo. "So we needn't worry about it. We live now."

Hoolie replied, "Just because it's from long ago doesn't make it useless. If Gepetto is everything he says, his words apply forever."

"Aw," said the gorilla, "I'm having a good time as it is. I don't need Gepetto to muss things up for me."

There were numerous arguments back and forth. Some toys sided with Hoolie. Others agreed with the lion, the hippo, and the gorilla and simply ignored it, even though the letter warned them gravely about the peril of rejecting its contents. Hoolie threw up his arms. "I don't understand this. Gepetto just wants us to learn to live in peace and to be like him. What's so bad about that?"

The monkey said, "It interferes with things, that's all. I'd rather do it my way."

"Well, at least you're honest." Hoolie walked away with some who agreed with him, but they were saddened by the response. They decided to continue reading the letter and thinking about it. They even began meeting to discuss it each morning.

They found Gepetto's wisdom on every imaginable subject. No situation ever arose where they couldn't look into the letter and find counsel on the problem. The letter brought them great hope. There were so many disagreements and fights in the toy shop that they often tired of it all. But Gepetto's letter assured him that there would someday be life beyond the toy shop.

As Hoolie and his friends studied the letter, a strange thing happened. They each began to change. Each became kinder, more understanding, more loving, and bolder than the other toys in the shop. Their words lightened many loads and encouraged each other.

Still, most of the toys scoffed. They noticed the changes in Hoolie and his friends, but they laughed about it. "Hoolie's become a goody-goody," they said. Some took advantage of him.

One day an incredible thing happened. Gepetto came back. Many of the toys were shocked and dismayed. Some even tried to hide. But Gepetto called them all together and asked them what each had done about his letter and his words. He found out everything.

Finally, Gepetto closed the toy shop and put all the useless toys into one of the closets. Then he took Hoolie and his friends and made a new toy shop, more resplendent and beautiful than the one they'd lived in.

Yet, when they entered it, they found that it wasn't a toy shop at all but a whole new world.

Something even more amazing had happened. When all the toys gathered together before Gepetto, they noticed a shining, a glory, a perfection about one another. Hoolie and his friends looked at each other and then at Gepetto.

"Why, we've become just like Gepetto!" cried Hoolie.

There was a great cry of praise, and, as Gepetto led them in song, they danced and shouted and played like the song would never end.

10
A Devilish Strategy

Memo

TO: Lucifer
FR: Grin
RE: David, presently king of Israel

You are correct in your criticisms of the situation. David has retired five different deceivers, the last one in only a week. We finally put a committee on him several eons ago. Koot had been doing fine with King Saul, stoking that jealousy and anger, but the old king seemed utterly unable to nab the twerp and dispatch him permanently. We're certain this is because the Enemy has been giving him special protection (the hedge, as you know). However, we're making efforts to penetrate it, and success is promised at any moment. Will keep you informed.

Update

TO: Lucifer
FR: Grin
RE: The cave ploy

The committee thought they had David trapped when the king came into the cave, relieved himself, and fell asleep. Even David's own men demanded his death. But David refused. Some nonsense about not touching the Lord's anointed. Do these bipeds ever get over the Enemy's preposterous superstitions?

We figured a stiff murder rap would bring his soul in, but he ran straight back to the Enemy's Word, wouldn't give in, and left the king to himself. (We did manage to get him to cut off a slice of the king's robe, and the garment was rendered beyond repair, but Saul isn't known as a sharp dresser and didn't care.)

Anyway, we threw the committee into the pit for an eon or two just to teach them a lesson, though I'm not sure what. We'll think of something.

The David problem is growing worse. He's writing up a psalm storm, and we're quite convinced the Enemy will soon be using these ditties as part of His (so-called) inspired Word. The less of that there is, the better. So we'd better can him quick. Perhaps a whole board of demons would help.

Tella-Crone Message

A CALL FROM: Lucifer
TO: Grin

Put together a board of Hell's finest, and bring the fish in. I'd like to dine on David's soul at my birthday feast.

Update

TO: Lucifer
FR: Grin

I have some wonderful news for you. The board we selected consisted of Foo (who deceived several potentates), Higglesplit (who first discovered the lust strategy), Geargrit, and Zob (whom you may remember as developing gluttony in bipeds during the Egyptian period). These sages, full of deception and guile, trundled out Bathsheba.

As you know, David has quite a reputation as a lover. After he became king he put the hustle on all the girls simply by adding them to his harem. So our sages faced a difficult state of affairs. The board had to search far and wide simply to find a woman pretty enough to turn his head. Finding one married to someone else was doubly difficult, for he'd taken up every beautiful lady for a hundred furlongs. But they found their number in Bathsheba. And what a number she was! (From a biped point of view, of course. As far as we're concerned, she was nothing but plate meat.)

As you suggested, we struck when David was bored, not working, and lonely. It was also the beginning of spring, and you know well what happens to those hot-blooded Semites in that season. In addition, he'd just gotten up—having stayed in bed all day. She was doing her best to be noticed. (Her husband, being off at war and rather holy, had become tiresome.)

While the king was up on his roof, he noticed the comely mistress as she bathed. Of course, his first thought was that he shouldn't look, but Higglesplit wisely suggested, "One look won't hurt."

The look accomplished, David couldn't help but keep looking. How easily these bipeds are snared with their eyes!

Nevertheless, his spiritual wits were still about him, and he reminded himself of the Enemy's commandment. ("You shall not commit adultery.") But Higglesplit countered with brilliance. "Maybe she's not married, and what a fine addition she'd be to your entourage. Shouldn't you find out?" (Please note, my lord, how we're applying to the letter your suggestions from your Memo on Deception.) The rake agreed and inquired who this woman was.

Then he discovered she was married and almost passed it all off. But Foo got into it then and said, "She is beautiful, isn't she—more so than any of the others, don't you think? You really ought to get a closer look!" (By the way, I have tried this strategy on a number of overweight rabbis. If I can get them to take a look into the food pot and get a whiff of fig pudding or lamb chop, I can usually have them gorging themselves in moments.)

We were sure that the Enemy would intercede at this point, but strangely, He was silent. This is a new one that bears further investigation. There may be times when He stops arguing with His subjects and lets them make their decisions without pressuring them. This may be prime tempt time for us. Of course, this may only be the case in His more mature saints. But apparently, He wants them to learn to choose right on their own, without incessant altercations with Him.

At any rate, with David staring at this fair damsel and himself virtually on fire, one thought kept banging away in his brain: "You know God's commandment. You can't have her. You can't commit adultery."

That's when Zob came into his own. He said, "But you're the king. Here you are, you've had a bad day, the rest of the harem has been complaining and nagging. You need some refreshment, some comfort. You don't have to put up with this nonsense about her being married. You're the king. Anyone would understand."

I tell you, the lad was nodding his head at this point!

Higglesplit fired in another shot, saying, "If you don't do it now, you'll never have another chance!" (Often that's just the touch we need!) And one more suggestion from Foo cached the loverboy: "Go ahead, call her in. You're not going to do anything. You just want to talk to her. Is that so bad?"

The fool sent for the woman and succumbed after a short conversation. The lady got pregnant (I'm amazed at how the board was able to get the timing right), and he got so upset that he had her husband murdered, then brought Bathsheba into his harem to "comfort" her. (Isn't it incredible the lies these bipeds dream up? Frankly, we hadn't even thought of that one.)

The lesson in it all, chief, is that the best deceptions start off as rather low key (as you've told us over and over). If we can think of our subject as descending a stairwell, we need be concerned only about getting him to take one step at a time. (Like they say in that old demonic proverb, a great sin always begins with the first step.) So our success, your awe-inspiring majesty, is actually your own, for it's your principles we've followed all along. You'll soon be savoring Holy Soul Delight!

Message

TO: Grin
FR: Lucifer

What's this about the profligate repenting? I'll have your horns if this one escapes and the Enemy pardons him. I'd better see his soul squirming at the next feast.

Report

TO: Lucifer
FR: Simpletune

Sir, I'm sorry to report that Grin has disappeared momentarily to Australia. Something about a study on the koala bear and its future use in fomenting idolatry in children. As for David, the Enemy is saying that He "forgave" him because he repented when the prophet Nathan confronted him. We know this "forgiveness" is just the Enemy's way of buying time. So our lawyers are confidently assaulting the throne every day, demanding release of the soul to our custody. So far, however, the Enemy has had the impudence to not even listen, saying it's all paid for. That, I'd like to see.

Anyway, we'll get our day in court, your worship, I assure you. The Enemy hasn't heard the last of us yet.

Purchase Order

TO: Simpletune
FR: Lucifer

Please prepare Grin's shadow for immediate consumption. If I can't dine on David, at least I can sup on a little rag of demon with my lunch.

11
Difference of Opinion

There were two scientists who constantly argued about whether God existed and had created the universe or not. One believed He had; the other didn't believe a Creator existed at all. They decided to perform an experiment. They went to a large plot of land, which they called, "God's Garden," and said, "If God is real, He'll turn this useless plot of ground into a great garden." The unbeliever told the believer to pray that God would do this, and he would watch and make calculations.

So they set up camp and waited. The believer prayed to God, and they both took readings on the garden.

One morning they woke up to find the rim of the garden ringed with beautiful roses of every sort and color. They were so big, redolent, and perfect that the believer knew that only God could have made them. He said, "See, God planted the roses."

But the unbeliever said, "How do we know that? What if you did it in the middle of the night? Or someone else came along? Or the wind blew them here?"

"But they grew up overnight," said the believer. "Only God could do that."

"Ha!" replied the unbeliever. "That's where I have you. I've been doing some investigations in the local library. It just so happens that one strain of roses has been evolving which grows very rapidly. What you have before you is merely another stage in the process of evolution."

The believer was thunderstruck, but he prayed again.

The next morning the whole garden was filled with vegetables—corn, potatoes, squash, beans. Again, they were all beautiful, larger than life, and not marred in any way. The two scientists walked through the garden, tasted the vegetables, and even sat down and had a fine meal.

Finally, the believer said to the unbeliever, "Now what do you say? Who could have done this but God?"

The unbeliever shook his head. "Do you see anybody? If He's here, why doesn't He show Himself? Besides, these aren't unusual vegetables. They only grew quickly. It's perfectly explainable."

"But how could they be so perfectly organized? Each row has no weeds, and the plants are spaced exactly right. How could this have happened if God didn't do it?"

The unbeliever just snorted. "I've made some calculations here, and I've found that given enough time, the garden could have organized itself this way by chance. Mark my words, if you search out in the world long enough, you'll find all sorts of gardens arranged every which way. This one just happened to come out this way. It's possible, according to some theories, that the ground just coughed these vegetables up. One day, ground. The next day, vegetables. They say that mutations can do virtually anything."

The believer was frustrated but decided to pray again.

The next morning a giant tree sat in the middle of the garden with a magnificent treehouse at its top. The believer awoke early, climbed the tree, and wandered about the treehouse. He'd never seen a place like it. It had every modern convenience. It was spacious. Twenty people could live in it comfortably.

He went down and invited his friend up to see it. Then he said, "Who else but God could have made such a place?"

But the unbeliever retorted, "If He's here, why doesn't He join us? Is He shy? I don't think God made this. In fact, it's not at all inconceivable that someone sneaked in here and did it overnight."

"Who?"

"Some of the townspeople. But my hunch is that an alien did it. The townspeople aren't smart enough for something like this."

"An alien? What kind of alien?"

"Someone from outer space. He probably sent down the seeds to grow such a place, and here you have it."

"Why not say that the alien was God then?"

"Because it wasn't. These things don't happen like that."

The believer was angry. "Look, your theory takes more faith than to believe God Himself did it!"

"From your point of view." He walked away and folded his arms.

The believer decided to pray at least once more.

The next morning he visited the treehouse, and an angel met with him. The angel was so perfect and resplendent that the believer immediately bowed in worship, but the angel stopped him. "I am not God. Do not worship me. Worship Him who gives all good gifts."

The believer did so, then carried on a lively discussion with the angel. Finally, he said, "Please stay until I get back with my friend. I want him to meet you." He ran down to get the unbeliever.

His friend just said, "You've had a hallucination. Your faith has made you mad." But the believer persuaded him to come and see.

They climbed up into the treehouse, and the angel was sitting in the easy chair and welcomed them both. The believer was so struck by the angel's power and perfection that he fell down and worshiped God, thanking Him for being so gracious. Then he stood up, pointed to the angel triumphantly, and said, "There! Only God could have servants like these. What do you say this time?"

The unbeliever only laughed. "Why it's just a little old man from the village. How much did you pay him to do this?"

The unbeliever went out in triumph and told all his fellow scientists that his friend had gone mad, and they decided to drum him out of the scientific organization.

The believer sat down with angel and asked, "When I saw you, I knew you were from God. Only God could have a servant like you. But when he saw you, he said you were only a little old man. Why?"

The angel smiled. "What did he see when the roses were put at the edge of the garden?"

"Ordinary roses. One more step in the process of evolution."

"And the vegetables?"

"Plain vegetables that grew fast."

"And the treehouse?"

"Just a simple treehouse like he made when he was a kid."

"So what did you expect him to see when he saw me?"

The believer sighed. He could see that what the angel said was true. But he said, "What if God Himself comes down and shows Himself to my friend? Wouldn't he believe then?"

"No," the angel said sadly. "If he didn't believe when he saw the roses or the vegetables or the treehouse or me, he won't believe when he sees God."

"Why not?"

"Because he doesn't want to. He willfully refuses."

"Why?"

The angel smiled. "Answer that question, and you will answer the question of all of history. We look into the books constantly to find the reason."

"And you haven't found one?"

"Not yet."

"When, then?"

"Eventually. But for now keep doing your job."

"What's that?"

"What you've always done. Tell others the truth. Live the truth. Worship Him who is truth."

"But what about my friend who doesn't believe?"

"There's nothing you can do about him. Just pray."

"Pray what?"

"That God Himself will intervene. That's your—and our—only hope."

The scientist nodded. Later, he went back out to the village. His friend had already aroused a group against him. Some were saying he should be stripped of his degree and his books destroyed.

But the scientist didn't mind. He simply continued talking to those who would listen. And some—a few—listened. He was grateful, knowing that God had worked and would continue to work through him, with him, and for him.

That was enough.

12

The Four Beggars

Four beggars sat about a fire sharing jokes and stories. One of them spoke of an enchanted forest. He said, "A prince lives there who gives fine gifts and a royal welcome to all who visit."

The other three were interested. They asked, "Why haven't you gone to his house?"

The first one threw up his hands and tossed his head. "I don't really feel like it."

Though the other three were skeptical, they decided to find out for themselves. "After all," said one, "the worst we can do is wear out our shoes. And they're already worn out."

So they set off in search of the enchanted wood. After a journey of many days, they came to a strange forest where birds sang and lit on their fingers, beavers gave firewood to travelers, and chipmunks brought nuts and berries to every stranger. The beggars were pleased. They made a fire and settled down for the night.

After all were asleep, the second beggar awoke at a sudden noise and noticed a light through the trees. He got up and walked toward it and soon discovered it was a great house, larger than he'd ever seen. He knocked on the door, and an ancient man greeted him, inviting him in. The beggar expected to find great treasures within. But instead, there was nothing but a large table with a huge loaf of bread upon it.

He asked the ancient man, "Where are the treasures?"

"Here," he said, pointing to the bread. "The greatest treasure of all—the bread of heaven."

The beggar snorted and headed for the door. He wakened the third beggar and told him he was heading home; the whole thing was a hoax.

But the third beggar decided to see for himself. He got up and headed toward the house. He was greeted similarly, and the ancient one showed him the bread. "The greatest bread our prince can offer," he said, explaining what it was.

The beggar inspected the bread closely and decided it might sell in the nearby town. He asked to take ten loaves with him.

"But don't you want to have some?" asked the old man.

"Nah," said the beggar. "I'd rather sell it and get money for it, so I can buy the good stuff."

The ancient one looked at him strangely, but the beggar just waved and went his way.

On his way out of the forest, he roused the fourth beggar and said, "Look, there's not much treasure here, but if you hurry, the bread looks like it might sell in town. I've got ten loaves. You can get your own."

The fourth beggar got up and went to the house. When the ancient one showed him the bread, he was instantly pleased. The ancient one gave him a piece. As he ate, it seemed that his mind and heart were filled with many things he'd never thought or known before. He also sensed a new, inner strength. "This is marvelous bread," he said. "I've never had anything like it."

"There is nothing like it," said the ancient one.

As they talked, the fourth beggar's eyes began seeing things he hadn't seen in the house before. Suddenly he jumped up, "Why, it's a treasure chest full of gold!" He ran across the room where a huge chest overflowed with gold.

"Yes," said the ancient one. "Take as much as you'd like."

The fourth beggar shivered with amazement. "I don't need much, so long as I'm here. I won't take any till it's time to leave."

"That's wise," said the ancient one with a nod.

They sat down together by the fire and shared their stories. In no time, the fourth beggar came to enjoy the ancient one's friendship. Then he noticed a huge pool of water on the other side of the room. "What's that?" he said, jumping up.

"Living water," said the ancient one.

"For drinking or bathing?"

"Both. And more."

"Please, I could use a bath," he said and took off his clothing.

The water was cool and warm at the same time. A delicious feeling of contentment came over him as he lay in it. "Do you swim in this yourself?"

"Of course," said the ancient one with a twinkle in his eye. "You certainly seem to be enjoying yourself."

As the fourth beggar looked around, he saw more treasures all over the room. Pearls. Banquet tables full of food. Birds singing tunes that calmed the soul. Clothing that was glory to behold and wear. And the room itself seemed to grow bigger. "Why it's a whole world of treasure," he said as he clambered out of the pool and toweled himself off.

"Yes," said the ancient one. "And you haven't seen the first hundredth of it."

For many days the beggar and the ancient one talked, supped, shared stories, and enjoyed one another. The beggar especially liked his stories about the great king who owned the house.

The beggar played with animals, had feasts with the ancient one, and dressed in the fine clothing. The ancient one gave him a huge diamond ring to wear on his left hand. "From the prince," he said.

One day it occurred to the beggar that he shouldn't hoard all the treasure for himself. "What should I do when I leave?" he asked the ancient one.

"Just tell everyone about the house here in the wood and the bread of heaven. In fact, bring them here yourself, and enjoy all the treasures together."

So the fourth beggar decided to head back to town and tell others about the house in the woods.

However, when he got to town and saw his other friends and began inviting people to come dine on the bread of life, there was much disagreement. The second beggar told people it was nothing and not to be concerned. The third beggar screamed about his interfering with his business. They ceased being friends. People joined with each beggar, and soon there were many different groups in town shouting about the others being charlatans and liars.

Nonetheless, the fourth beggar ignored their taunts and continued to invite people to come taste the bread of life in the house in the forest. Many people came and ate the bread and partook of the treasures. But the beggar especially enjoyed the ancient one himself and his stories about the king. It seemed he learned every one of them by heart.

Then one day the ancient one approached the beggar, saying, "I must go on a long journey. Will you take care of the house? It's not mine, as you know, but the king's. All you must do is receive travelers, offer them the bread and treasures, and take care of things."

The beggar was overjoyed. But he said, "I'm only a beggar. How can this be?"

The ancient one laughed. "You're no longer a beggar, my son. You're the new master of the enchanted wood. It's all yours until the king himself returns."

The beggar trembled and was silent for a long time. "I never thought anything like this could happen to me."

The ancient one smiled. "Anything can happen to him who believes and obeys. I also was once a beggar like you."

The beggar stared at the ancient one a moment. Then he smiled. Somehow he knew it was the truth, almost as though he'd known it all along.

He watched the ancient one walk off down the road, then began preparing the bread for whatever travelers might come. "They'll have it just as I did," he said and sat in the main room waiting, eager for the first guest to arrive.

13
Test

Among the artifacts in the recent excavations at the Pit was discovered this correspondence from Scrubdub, a demon, to his disciple, Loopole.

Dear Loopole:

Your astonishment is revealing, my child. I told you that our lawyers and agents, even Lucifer himself, are continually demanding opportunity to test a Christian to show his true self. Your lawyer won this occasion for you after years of proofs, briefs, indictments, and arguings. So we do with all "saints." We repeatedly assert to the Enemy that if He'll let down His wretched hedge and give us a chance to assault freely, we'll prove once and for all that every one of them is a clod deserving just and final committal to our sphere of ingestion.

If you look again into the Enemy's Book, you'll see several occasions on which our Father below asked and gained permission to "sift" a man. Job is a good example. So is Peter (Luke 22:31-34). Lucifer even won an opportunity against the son of God Himself in the wilderness. As you know, he was so befuddled by our magnificent Lord that he resorted to that banal tactic of Scripture-prattling and quacking Bible quotes. Though our Lord was prepared, the son tricked him into departing by using the old "Begone, Satan" ploy, and, as you know, Lucifer hates that name. He decided at the time that if the son was going to resort to name-calling to push him off, then he'd have nothing to do with him.

Of course, don't think that Job and Peter passed their respective tests. As you can see, Job was reduced to a complaining justice-demander, and Peter failed so miserably that he denied he even knew Jesus to slave girls. Once again, our Father's contention was proved: even the Enemy's choicest will waver and fall in the face of our master's onslaught.

Just the same, you've been given a real opportunity with Jenkins. You must make the most of it. Don't be bothered that the Enemy has placed several limitations on you—that you can't harm him physically, that the duration of the test is dependent on his will, and that you can't prevent the church from helping him. To be sure, the Enemy is unfair. What he gives with his right hand, he always takes back with his left. But if you think through what you will do, you shall not only have your man for breakfast and lunch but also for supper and a mid-hell snack.

Scrubdub

Loopole:

I'm glad you asked. Strategy is important. How will we go about this little caper?

First, note that Jenkins has been thinking himself quite spiritual and mature of late. Glump reported to me that he was recently musing that they'll soon offer him a position on the church leadership council. This attitude is excellent, for it manifests pride. Pride always prevents a man from depending on the Enemy.

Second, you've properly planted a vague and caricatured image of us in his mind. It's always sensible to keep his mind on things of earth rather than things above. As a result, he's not only unaware of the Enemy's presence, but he's also unaware of yours. He thinks you're able only to attack his mind, and he's convinced he can ward off any of your suggestions with a splash of common sense. Thus, he's underestimated us and forgotten the power of the Enemy's Word. Now: how do you attack?

Remember several things:

1. Subtlety. Since he's underestimated you, he's also underestimated the subtlety of your attack. Thus, you want to plot out clearly what he'll be most unprepared for.

For instance, I once destroyed a young man who was sports-oriented and highly competitive. He gave a vibrant testimony before various sports circles and was useful to the Enemy. But he began to love his testimony more than his Lord. Then the Enemy gave us our opportunity. I was able to engineer a traffic accident, and we sent the squeak into a truck. He ended up hospitalized and temporarily paralyzed. I had him carefully caulked into a state of blessed bitterness for months and even hoped the lad would go the way of complete agnosticism in the end. (However, our ruthless Enemy clipped me off in the midst of it and sent a young man to disciple him. In no time, he was "giving thanks in all things." Alas, I was unable to return him to his former state.)

The point is, hit him where he least expects it. Strike an area where he thinks he's strong. That's where you'll find him less dependent on the Enemy.

2. Surprise. Don't mistake what I mean here. I'm not referring to the kind of attack that leaps out of the dark and pounces on him. You don't even want him to be surprised. What you want is that he be bitterly disappointed. He must feel that God has let him down. He must think that everything he has believed is foolishness. He must become convinced that nothing in the Book works—the promises in vain, the commands impossible, the stories ridiculous. You must lead him into such a hole that when he looks up and about, he'll see nothing but darkness. When you have him there, he'll go one of two ways: give up the faith and speed on through life believing his religious period was mere whim; or learn to persevere.

3. The slow slide. Again, don't get him going too fast. There's always the chance he'll jolt alert in the face of it. First, you want disobedience to the Enemy's commands. Then distrust of the Enemy himself. Finally, the disowning of the Enemy.

Keep your head. Don't let him crack your nerve with scripture-quoting. And don't be looking for the grand heist. Ease him down, and you'll find he'll roast just as savory.

Scrubdub

Loopole:

Even now I can taste Jenkins basted and broiled. Your strategy is brilliant. I've often used this tactic myself.

I received word that you struck Jenkins initially with anxiety and worry about his work situation. This led to some inner emotional convulsions, which, I understand, you aggravated by upsetting the chemical balance in his body. This has led to a deep depression. Though he went to a doctor, and though the doctor is supposed to be a Christian, he has no understanding of the spiritual matter of the "sifting of a saint." Therefore, he had no idea that Jenkins had been given into our custody for the time being. Thus, though the doctor's trying to fight it using medication and other therapies, Jenkins's bleats and cries for answers have utterly mystified him.

I think it's wise for you to direct Jenkins to the question of why. Get him obsessed with the idea that if he can discover why all this is happening, he'll find an instant solution to the problem. The reason I say this is that we know he will never understand it in purely logical and human terms, but of course, those are the kind of terms he demands.

More important, the Enemy won't tell him why. (And I don't think you're planning on it, are you?) By miring him in a quag of questions, you fix him in mental muck and aggravation that will keep him depressed for months to come. And even if he did know why this is happening to him, it wouldn't provide the instantaneous solution he seeks.

Of course, you should offer Jenkins some fanciful explanations for his condition, such as, "You've committed some sin. If you could only find it and confess it, you'd be free." Or, "God is trying to teach you something. Once you learn the lesson, the trial will be over."

At the same time, I highly recommend that you reinforce his idea that this condition will last the rest of his life. (Isn't it interesting the way a biped will in one moment believe the trial will never end and in the next be praying fervently that it will end that hour?) Keep telling him, "This will never end," and, "You'll be like this forever—even in heaven."

What you want to do is lead Jenkins to "give up the faith." You might lead him into another religion, at which time you can free him from his depression. Or, you can simply bring him to the conclusion that Christianity is bunk, and he'll have to find his own way in the world. Either way, you'd have your man.

You might reread Job to gain more insight, but don't let Jenkins do so. And keep him away from the Psalms. You wouldn't want him discovering that some of their great ones felt exactly as he does now.

Scrubdub

Loopole:

This is no time for gloating. You haven't got your man. He isn't dead yet, is he? It's only after a person has died unrepentant and faithless that he's secure.

Simply that Jenkins is questioning his faith in ways never before witnessed is no cause for feasting. The Enemy is allowing you to put him through a period of suffering. If you do not properly direct him, this could lead to refining and spiritual transformation that you will shudder to sniff.

To be sure, Jenkins is wondering why this is happening. He has long conceived of the Enemy as One who always gives joy, peace, and hope in circumstances. But this period of emotional turmoil has rocked his faith, or so he thinks. In actuality, it has only shaken out the dregs you had been carefully putting into his milk.

What had you been telling him? That all will be well if he just trusts the Enemy? That nothing ever goes wrong in true Christians' lives? That all he must do is pray and things will be made right? That the Enemy always wants him happy and joyous? That was good as far as it went. But the reason we plant such ideas in our subjects is to head them off. That is, if we get a biped to believe the above things, he'll often give up the faith when calamity strikes.

However, it can also go the other way. The Enemy can use a trial to screen out the theological gunk we've crammed into his cranium. The result is a cleaner, more committed disciple than ever. How, then, can you combat this possibility?

You must note that the Enemy has allowed him to experience something he is utterly incapable of overcoming on his own: depression. Though he goes to doctors, does what they say, memorizes Scripture, studies, prays, and seeks counsel, he is stymied. Nothing works! He's still in the same dark and miserable condition.

Now he's undergoing such fierce doubts that he actually asked his wife if God really exists. I know you cheered when he did that, but you should be alarmed. He might discover the grim truth that God's existence is real, apart from any good or bad feelings he has at a given moment—and that he should depend on what the Book says, rather than on his senses, mind, emotions, or mood.

What it boils down to is this: Jenkins is living with several important misconceptions, which you must keep advancing.

The first misconception is that simply practicing spiritual disciplines insures that he'll always be happy, fruitful, and close to the Enemy. The result is that he's come to trust in his spiritual disciplines more than in the Enemy himself.

So you see one reason the Enemy has allowed this condition. He wants to wean Jenkins away from love of his habits (spiritual, though they may be) and encourage him to love Him. If Jenkins comes to understand that it is the Enemy himself—not the habits—who satisfies, then he will seek the Enemy all the more determinedly.

The second misconception he has is that since he feels useless—isn't sharing his faith consistently, is not leading people to Christ, and so on—somehow he has failed the Enemy. Little does he know that the Enemy often renders His disciples ineffective (in the sense that they do not accomplish many visible, tangible things for His kingdom) in order to draw them closer to Himself and to perfect them through suffering. This ultimately yields a more effective disciple. But you must keep Jenkins from perceiving this. Keep him focusing on what he's *not* doing for the Enemy, rather than on the fact that he's learning more about the Enemy.

The third misconception is his conviction that the Enemy couldn't possibly want him to be going through this. This creates a paradox in his mind. On the one hand, he's convinced the Enemy doesn't want this to be happening. On the other hand, it quite obviously is happening. Thus, he is led to the conviction that the Enemy must be powerless, loveless, or nonexistent. You want to reinforce this idea. It might lead him out of Christianity altogether.

Scrubdub

Loopole:

Your last letter appalls me, and I can see the situation has gone beyond your control without your even realizing it. I thought you were ready for this, but now I'm not sure. Our negotiations with the Enemy specified that only you could attack Jenkins. Though we can provide advice, we are impotent at this point to make proper mincemeat out of this quack.

Here are your greatest errors.

You say (in some of the purplest terms I've seen from any demon), "The woolyhaired tweet has been poring over the Scriptures steadily in search of 'the deep dark secret verse.' Ha! That will zip him out of his circumstances in twiddly doo. Little does he know there isn't a secret verse—Ha ha! And even if there were, he'd miss it because he's the most self-pitying, piteous, putrid priss I've seen in months—Ha ha ha!"

Aside from your grammar and self-congratulation, you seem to have missed the point. So there isn't a secret verse? So he hopes there is? So he'll be disappointed when he fails to find it? The thing you have missed is that he's reading his Bible like a Gulag prisoner looking for slivers of meat. He goes to it every day full of anticipation and hope. Even though at the end of the day he's discouraged and limp, he's learning what the Book says, you dolt! He's meditating on it, digesting it, grasping and grabbing and scrabbling and racing through it in search of something—anything—to get him out of his depression. He cares nothing for magazines, tomes, digests, how-to books, or any other paraphernalia. He's actually become convinced that the Book alone has the answer.

Have you gone insane? Put him onto Maslow. Give him Freud. Get him reading *The Post*. Anything else, but put a stop to this steady intake of truth. The man is on the verge of discovering that the Book is the only thing in the world worth trusting, even if he feels miserable about it.

You make the same mistake with prayer. You say, "He goes to the Enemy daily, pleading, moaning, threatening, begging for relief, for an end. It borders on hilarity. He's become a one-subject pray-er: 'Oh, Lord, please help me. I can't take this another minute. Please get me through this hour.'"

It grieves my hate to think that you revel in this.

Did it ever occur to you that though he's not praying much for others, and though his prayers have become self-centered, the fact of the matter is that he is praying? Furthermore, he's learning fervency in prayer, desperation, fire. He's no longer trying to win the world. He just wants to make it through one more day and not desert his Lord.

Do you see the horror of this? The man is communing with the Enemy on a level and in ways he never before considered. The Enemy has become his only hope, you fool! He's begun to see the Enemy as the first one to go to with a need, and the only one to go to. He's discovering his mortality! He's realizing that without God he's nothing. I can't believe these things have escaped you. I tell you, I had to fight last week to keep you on the case. There are demons in high places who want your throat, Loopole. I'm standing by you. But I tell you, I can't hold back a tornado.

You say, "He feels miserable. He's at the brink of suicide every day. He looks at the gas oven and thinks that would be the way to do it, if it came to that. The Enemy's presence is gone from his psyche."

"The Enemy's presence"! Do you have any idea what the Enemy's presence is? You're just like Jenkins. You conceive of it as some kind of garment, soft and fuzzy, that enwraps him in furry puffs of joy and peace all the day. You think it's a happy little squeal he gets in his brain when everything is going right.

98

How piteous.

In reality, Loopole, the Enemy's presence is not seen but understood, not always felt with the emotions but held in the heart like rock. They think of his presence as a child would, walking through a dark woods with his father. But the Christian who entrusts his life to the truth knows that the Enemy is not only with him, but goes before him, behind him, over him, and under him. The Enemy not only holds his hand but controls every twig and leaf he passes. You are seeing the Enemy's presence as a shield. But we know it is like a fortress the size of the whole earth.

Right now Jenkins thinks the Enemy has lost control. But if you allow him to draw near to him, pray, and read the Book as he's doing, he'll soon be the kind of Christian who thinks nothing about feelings. He'll be staking his life on truth, not on passing fancies. He'll be trusting what the Book says, even when you're telling him the opposite.

Wise up, demon. No more of Bible study, prayer, and pleadings for intercession. Let me hear that the man is getting drunk or going to rock concerts or buying new jeans to ease his pain.

Scrubdub

Loopole:

The man is "resigned to his condition"? Resigned? Is that all? Well, I had to learn the facts from Scog since you wouldn't tell all. What you should've said is that Jenkins has submitted himself entirely to the Enemy's sovereignty. Not that he's simply accepted Jesus as his Lord. As you know, he did that (as they all must do) at the very beginning. But that original decision was verbal. This is from the heart.

Apparently, though you've been allowed to keep Jenkins in this state of depression for more than a year with no visible change, he's finally given up fighting and has told the Enemy that he'll obey, love, and serve Him regardless of whether He ever blesses him again. Scog said the man got down by his bed and wept. He provided me with a transcript of the whole wretched prayer: "Lord, I can't change my condition. So I'm willing to accept it. Whatever You want me to do I'll do, even

99

if my pain never lifts. I'll obey You, worship You, follow You, and love You as long as I live. [The very words are causing me to choke, my little friend.] I know now that You are God and that there is nowhere else to go. I cast myself at Your feet and only ask You to give me the grace to keep on going. Thank You for hearing me. Thank You for allowing me to go through this. And thank You for as long as it lasts."

In a word, you've lost your man, Loopole. He's learned true submission. It will not be long before he's seeking to obey everything in the Book. For that reason, I'll make this short. You're not to be cast into the pit. No, we have better uses for the likes of you. Actually, we're leaving you on the case. We'll let you witness every day the growth this young twerp is going to experience. You're going to find out what it's like to have to be around one of their "true saints." Have a ball, my friend.

Scrubdub

14
Comments on the Parables

The Good Samaritan

*A certain Samaritan, who was on a journey, came upon him;
and when he saw him, he felt compassion.... and bandaged
up his wounds. (Luke 10:33-34)*

> Compassion.
> The stoop of a listening father.
> The touch and wink
> of a passing nurse.
> The gnarled fingers
> of a grandmother
> steadying a swing.
> The clench of a surgeon's teeth
> as he begins his cut.
> The open hand and pocketbook
> of a traveling Samaritan.
> The dew of heaven
> on dry lips.

The Great Supper

*A certain man was giving a big dinner, and he invited many.
... But they all alike began to make excuses. (Luke 14:16, 18)*

Because he bought a piece of land,
he didn't go to the great feast of God.
Because he didn't go to the feast,
he went out to inspect the land.
Because he inspected the land,
he knew he'd make a million.
Because he knew he'd make a million,
he made millions.
Because he made millions,
he ruled lands, businesses, people.
Because he ruled so many,
they elected him president.
Because he became president,
his word was their command.
Because his word was their command,
he was honored, respected, and loved.
He had everything he wanted—
wine, women, song, and roses.

They used the roses at his funeral.

And because he had so much,
it was a great funeral.
Almost as great as a great feast.

The Seed Growing Secretly

The kingdom of heaven is like a man who casts seed upon the soil; and goes to bed at night and gets up by day, and the seed sprouts up and grows—how, he himself does not know. (Mark 4:26-27)

You push in a plug,
flick the switch, and light claps
into a room. Stupendous.

You slide in the key, twist it,
and turn the knob. The door opens.
Amazing.

You nestle a kernel in dirt,
cover it, loam it, guard it.
Three months later, you're licking your lips
and devouring cobs. Almost a miracle.

You plead with a friend,
show him the texts, weep, pray.
His eyes are empty.
You go away broken.

But one day he comes to you,
his eyes shining, his face creased
and edged at the laugh places. His joy
is deep as Jerusalem.
You ask him, "How?"
He can't explain. "It was this and that,
and your word so long ago."

You're astonished.
You don't understand.
But you rejoice like a child,
dancing in puddles
and leaping in sunshine.

The Lost Coin

*What woman, if she has ten silver coins and loses one coin,
does not light a lamp and sweep the house and search carefully until she finds it? (Luke 15:8)*

This isn't just a parable.
I've seen it.

My fiancee put her diamond ring
on the edge of the bathtub
as she took her shower.
Not what I'd do, but it's her ring.

She pulled back the curtain
and let go the waterburst.
After washing, she stepped out, toweled up, ambled
back to her room, checked herself
in the mirror. Felt her ring finger.
Instantly remembered.
The chill that shot through her
could have cooled Nigeria.

She ran into the bathroom,
bent down by the tub. Nothing.
Checked the floor. Bare.
Felt the drain. Soapsuds alone.
Looked under the counter,
down the toilet, over the soap dish.
Gone.
It was either a diamond ring thief,
the dog, the drain,
or a mad spinster.
Many tears. Many cries.

She called me. Desperation personified.
I almost gave her a lecture.
But I held back.
That's when her mom told her she'd picked it up.
A little lesson in engagement ring management.
Many tears. Many cries.

She said to me, "Let's celebrate.
Take me out to dinner."
We went.
She celebrated, just like the lady
in the parable. (I paid.)

The Lost Sheep

What man among you, if he has a hundred sheep and has lost one of them, does not leave the ninety-nine in the open pasture, and go after the one which is lost? (Luke 15:4)

Have you ever been lost?
When somehow Mom gets preoccupied
with the price of spaghetti at the supermarket
and drops your hand?
When you look up, the shelves start closing in,
and strange people with strange breath
huddle around asking your name?

When you're late and you scurry down the hall
on your first day in high school, and you arrive
breathless—in the wrong classroom—
and kids are snickering and you're convinced
you'll flunk and never graduate, never
get a job, never muddle through life
with happiness, let alone dignity?

When you're staring into a restaurant window
where steaks sputter on the grill,
and the hungry child on your hip cries,
"Why can't we have some, Mommy? Why won't
they give us any?"
And you can only tell him to hush?

When one day a friend dies or you have a close
call on the highway or your heart stops
just a moment, and in your deepest soul
you know one day you will die,
you will explode into that dark,
and nothing within you offers assurance,
nothing says with finality it will be all right;
you can face it, you can triumph—
no, everything is saying you will face God,

you will be judged,
you will be condemned.

That is the moment you are ready to say yes
when the Good Shepherd comes upon you
and offers to carry you out and back
into eternity.

The Ten Virgins

All those virgins arose, and trimmed their lamps. And the fool-
ish said to the prudent, "Give us some of your oil, for our
lamps are going out." (Matthew 25:7-8)

Any time you get ten virgins
after the same fellow
there's bound to be trouble.

One's so busy arranging her face
she simply runs out of lamplight.
A second's on the phone
making powderpuff lipcracks.
The third's checking her luggage—
veils, compacts, stockings—you know—
and checking them twice.
The fourth's on a shopping spree
getting ready for heaven.
And the fifth's got stars in her eyes.
Just slipped her mind gazing at his photo.

Now those other five—
the ready ones—what were they?
CPAs?
Engineers?
Lawyers?
Career types?

It doesn't say.
But they did know how
to use those lamps.

The Friend at Midnight

*Suppose one of you shall have a friend, and shall go to him at
midnight, and say to him, "Friend, lend me three loaves..."
and from inside he shall answer and say, "Do not bother me."
(Luke 11:5-7)*

It's hard. A man praying is
the nub tip of grass
jammed against rock, craving only a break,
a cleft, just a glimpse-hint of sunlight.

It's pain. A man praying is
the chick, beak sore and cramped,
hammering at the shell, each tick
a jab to the ribs, each tack
a crimp in a joint.

It's sweat. A man praying is
the last ember of winter fire,
the flame quivering in the tint-blue air,
suspended between torch and ash,
dream and doubt, ask and answer.

See him pray.
Scrutinize the lips,
the slow exhale of words,
the thistles among the question marks.

See him hope. See him despair.
See the joy break
with the tears.

The Talents

His master answered and said to him, "You ... ought to have put my money in the bank, and on my arrival I would have received my money back with interest." (Matthew 25:26-27)

If only I were Beethoven.
I'd snatch the stars out of their slants
and write down the melodies,
call them *Starlight Sonatas*.

If only I were Lewis.
I'd take philosophy, science, faith, and joy,
weave them together in cords of clause,
and write down hope like buttons of fire.

If only I were Rockefeller.
I'd fling dimes and dollars, set up foundations,
give to the poor,
help the trodden.
If only.

Alas, I'm not Beethoven.
Can't hold a tune.
And Lewis thought thoughts I'd blow a circuit
trying to think.
As for Rockefeller,
I can't even turn a tenner.

I couldn't do much with my little tunes,
my verses from John,
and my piggy bank layaway.
I'll just stash it all away in a cookie jar.
Maybe it'll turn into some macaroons.

The Lost Son

While he was still a long way off, his father saw him, and felt compassion for him, and ran and embraced him, and kissed him. (Luke 15:20)

The story begins with a boy gone bad.
Faces in the audience light up.

The boy takes full advantage
of his father, an ancient, kindly man.
He wants the inheritance. Everything.
Faces grimace.
"An upstart," someone says.
"Horsewhip him ... teach him some manners."
Some young men smile,
but they all wait, eyes fixed
on the face of Jesus.

The father lets him go
after giving everything,
the whole inheritance: the gold, the silver,
the favorite horse, the treasured cloak, the ring.

Faces show surprise.
"This father's a fool," someone whispers.
"The son's a cheat."
But they bend forward to hear.

He spends it all on prostitutes,
wine, gambling, the best hotels.
Loose living.
An old man looks down at his friend
and winks.
"He should have invested it,"
he says. "This one's a fool."
Heads nod in agreement.

Soon the boy hits bottom.
Nothing left. He ends up slopping pigs.
Faces flinch, stunned.
Some smile. "He got what he deserved,"
an old man says. "A good story."

The boy remembers home.
The feasts. The plenty. The laughter.
He sits and weeps, his head in his hands.
He decides to return, to ask for a bed
in the barn. Someone laughs. "A twist,"
he says. Faces show intrigue.

The boy comes home, hands gritty,
legs scarred. He is penniless, ragged,
wasted, a scarecrow.
Listeners are laughing now.
Revenge, they think. The disowning.

But no.
The old man sees him on the road
from his chair on the porch where he has sat,
waiting each day. He recognizes the walk,
the long hair, the shoulders. He jumps up
and stumbles out to him, his heart thumping,
his eyes wet. He runs to the boy;
the boy stands, head down.

The old man
gathers him into his arms and holds him long,
so long, and he weeps.
Faces are stern now, eyes slit.
"This father's still a fool," they murmur.

But they wait.
The boy begins his speech, but the old man
has suddenly gone deaf. He throws a cloak
over the boy's rags, pulls off his last

and best ring, slides it onto the boy's finger,
and calls for the servants.
"Kill the fatted calf!" he shouts.
"We'll have a feast."
Many shake their heads.

A bitter, elder son
refuses to speak to his lost brother.
He stomps off,
angry, cursing.
Some faces nod. But most are gray,
lips pressed white.
Eyes flame.
Some stand to go.

Nothing has gone right in this story.
They stalk off. "A bad story,"
one says. "Stupid," says another.
"Not one of His best."

But some from the crowd linger—
a prostitute, tax gatherer, thief, liar.
They glance at Jesus furtively.
They wait. Then approach shyly,
slowly. One by one they fall at His feet
and weep
for joy.

The Pharisee and the Publican

*The Pharisee stood and was praying thus to himself, "God, I
thank Thee that I am not like other people." (Luke 18:11)*

All whites to the left side of the room, please.
Everyone else out.

Next, all Americans. You stay.
The rest can go.

111

Now, Republicans. Everyone else may go.

Let's see now. Yes, conservatives.
Hold your post. Everyone else . . .
Oh, you know.

Born-again Christians.
Of course you stay. Don't be silly.
You don't know?
Well, stand over there. We'll see
as we go along.

Creationists?
Twenty-four-hour days, of course.
Well, don't get all worked up about it.
Just go.

Now, Baptists.
"Both ways?"
Well, stay for now.

Evangelicals.
No arguing, please. They all stay.

Neos, fundies . . . Oh.
Well, get that one out.
(I never could abide those partial inerrantists.)

Premillennialists?
What? Don't ask silly questions.
Look it up in the dictionary.
Look, if you don't know, you aren't. Go.

Well, then, Calvinists?
Of course the Reformed tradition.
Oh, we don't recognize those four or fewer pointers.
You may go.

"Thank you"?

Let's see, against abortion,
for capital punishment, against prayer
in schools.

Now we're getting somewhere.
Supports prison reform, feeds the hungry,
justice for the oppressed, and doesn't smoke,
drink, or chew.
"Dancing?" No, I didn't say anything about dancing.
"Movies?" Yes, stay. Don't be ignorant.
"Cards and games?" Oh, come on!
This is the twentieth century.

OK, just two more.
"Takes long walks."
"Jogging?" Get out. Out.

Finally, has a regular quiet time.
Don't give me that look.
Every day.

OK, who's left?
Where is everybody?
Good heavens, what is
this world coming to?

The Rich Fool

*But God said to him, "You fool! This very night your soul is
required of you." (Luke 12:20)*

His dreams are the pot at the end
of the ticker tape.
His dreams are mines,
spasms of gold and lovely lucre.
His dreams are the stuff of goose flesh
and duck down, feather pillows
and embossed envelopes. He paints

with the colors of dawn and destiny.
He sings with the melodies of blueprint
and master plan. He cries with tears
of opal and onyx. He punches in,
knuckles down, and piles up.

And one day he's rich—
rich beyond dreams, summer, spring,
and winter moonshine; rich beyond
dime novels and Austrian chateaus,
yachts and restaurants. He's free
of worry, scurry, and flinch.
Gone: the shudders.
Gone: the willies.
Gone: the creeps, creepers, and peepers.
Even winter loses its edge.
Morning comes with his eggs up and easy.
The parakeets skeet.
The paramount mounts.
The paradox docks nothing and no one.

And that morning when he lies breathless and cold,
his kids carve in his headstone,
"What a Daddy"
and go out and buy Babylon.

The Sower

And he spoke many things to them in parables, saying, "Behold, the sower went out to sow." (Matthew 13:3)

It's a rough business—sowing.
The inclement weather, the seasonal
lethargies, the cycles of monster harvest,
total loss, disappointment, trickle,
trifle, triumph, crash.
You never know what's next.

And the soil. The hardpack,
like drum skin, bounces a seed,
then lies under it like an unforgiving hand,
unwilling to clutch, to clasp, to grasp.

The rockstrewn, like broken shell in egg,
betrays. It promises a meal,
delivers grit. It extends a hand,
then casts a stone.

And the weedy soil,
so full of sex and seed,
is a prostitute, welcoming every lover.

Still, there's the good soil.
Brown, it clumps in the hand
and clings, wet, cool—dirt,
like lips and grass and beef
and feathers. You live for such soil.
You embrace it,
feed it,
walk in it without sandals,
grip it with your toes,
kneel in it and knead it.
You throw it in the air and laugh
and cry and pray.

Yet, you cast the seed
on all. And you pray.
You weep
and watch the mists
rise off the fields
as you walk. And you let your feet
sink deep.

The Pearl of Great Price

*The kingdom of heaven is like a merchant seeking fine pearls,
and upon finding one pearl of great value, he went and sold
all that he had, and bought it. (Matthew 13:45-46)*

First, you see it.
It glistens. Light floats
from its surface like mist.
You touch it: silk, the cheek
of a first daughter.
You caress it: roundness
like a lover's laughter.
You ask the price.
Your heart leaps, then falls.

You head home, pause,
look back, catch a glint of white.
You turn—once, twice, seven, ten
times. You go back.
You bargain, chew your lip, flinch,
plead. "What's the bottom,
dead bottom?" "Everything."
You storm away.

But again you're back.
You argue, pace, pound your fists
into palms. You review everything
a hundred times.

Finally, you pay: pocket change.
The car. The bank accounts and stocks.
Stamp collection. China, clothing,
furniture. Children. Wife.
Yourself.

It's yours.
You laugh.
Hold it up to the sun and weep.

Shout to neighbors.
You lie back.

No regrets.
No returns.
No end to the soft, quiet jubilation.

The Two Sons

[One son] said, "I will, sir"; and he did not go. And he came to
the second and said the same thing. But he answered and
said, "I will not"; yet he afterward regretted it and went. Which
of the two did the will of his father? (Matthew 21:29-31)

No Christian in his right mind says to God,
"I won't." "I refuse." "Find someone else."

We're subtle.
We pray about it.
We give a little more next Sunday.
We go witnessing twice in a week.
That makes us feel better
that we didn't do
what we were supposed to do.

Now, those second sons—
the nonsophisticates—
a little coarse on the surface,
saying, "Not me. Nope. No way."
But in the end they come through.

I'll go with one of them
anytime.

The Laborers in the Vineyard

Did you not agree with me for a denarius? Take what is yours and go your way, but I wish to give to this last man the same as to you. (Matthew 20:13-14)

You come to expect it:
the square deal; the honest wage;
the right bucks for the right hours.

So you look at the boss through a red squint,
a blue snort, and a black ball.
"We'll strike," you say. "We'll break him.
We'll show him who's who. We'll get our rights."
And you fight.

You scratch, kick, snarl, and curse
for every inch of break, every yard of benefit,
every centimeter of wage and privilege.
You expect him to fight, too.
You have words. You exchange blows.
You come to the table, make your demands,
sit tight. You haggle, bend, break.

You chirp, whistle, spit, and fume.
You shake hands. You go to work. You bloom.

And then he gives everyone the same wage,
the same cut, the same slice of the sky.
No one gets less than he deserves.

But many get more.

You're mad.
You worked longer, harder.
Bore the heat of the day.
You should get more—even though
you agreed to this price. You've been slimed,
you say. Hammered. Ridden down the primrose

gangplank and dunked.
You've been wangled and dangled,
bongoed and plopped. It's unfair.
Crude. You could have booed.

But the boss is adamant. No returns.
So you smoke your cigarettes.
You won't work for him.
Won't even look his way.
You'll show him.
Hate him right down to the end,
even if it takes
eternity.

The Two Debtors

A certain moneylender had two debtors: one owed five hundred denarii, and the other fifty. When they were unable to repay, he graciously forgave them both. Which of them therefore will love him more? (Luke 7:41-42)

The first one
borrowed big to make it fabulous.
Ended up with a slack sack
and a sad face.

And the second one
borrowed small to make it medium.
But even minimum payments wore him down.
It's an accountant's nightmare, this world.

The first one throttles his pride,
falls to his knees, and crawls to the banker.
Amazingly, he's forgiven.

The second stumbles out,
pleads insolvency, and gets the same treatment.

(I wish this man were my banker,
but it only happens in fiction.)

Which one loves more?
The one forgiven most,
obviously.

Which one loves less?
I'm not sure.
Does the one who loves less
actually love at all?

The Unmerciful Servant

*Summoning him, his lord said to him, "You wicked slave, I
forgave you all that debt because you entreated me. Should
you not also have had mercy on your fellow slave, even as I
had mercy on you?" (Matthew 18:32-33)*

Mercy flows
from the springs of God
like blood from a mortal wound.
Blooms upon earth
like a flush
on a quiet woman's cheek.
Takes root and grows
when exposed to light and Son.
Only when men take it
and hoard it,
does it, like manna the day after,
rot and stink.

The Coin in the Fish's Mouth

*Go to the sea, and throw in a hook, and take the first fish that
comes up; and when you open its mouth, you will find a
stater. (Matthew 17:27)*

Simple story:
Citizens pay taxes—to insure national defense,
oil the bureaucracy.
Even though Jesus was exempt,
He'd better humor them. IRS agents
don't favor appeals to divinity.
So Peter is sent fishing.
The first grunt up should fill the bill.
Find the tax in its mouth.

But what fisherman worth his trotline
simply throws in a hook?
He's got to plan, scheme, dream.
Tie some flies. Mend a net.
He can't simply sashay down to the beach
and let his rod rip.

Furthermore, what fish sells out for sheer hook?
Worms, that's what fish want.
You've got to spit on it, dangle it,
wangle it. It takes time. Often hours.
Sometimes you can kill a whole day
without even a nibble.
But no fish worth his gills
springs for hook minus entree.

There's also this matter
of coin in fish's mouth.
What fish carries cache under tongue?
And why splurge for hook when he can afford
cricket? Or night crawler?
And what possible motive might move
this finny Carnegie from down under
to up top at risk of life and bank account?
This almost makes no sense.

But then,
nothing in the tax business ever does.

The Rich Man and Lazarus

*And he cried out and said, "Father Abraham, have mercy on
me, and send Lazarus ... to my father's house—for I have five
brothers—that he may warn them, lest they also come to this
place of torment." (Luke 16:24-28)*

Send to the teacher-brothers,
and make sure verb follows noun.
Tell them, tell them,
the cries of hell have no grammar.

Send to the stamp-brother.
Tell him the value of the early British
collection, and how it brings no rolls
on the tables of hell.

Send to the doctor-brothers.
Assure them there's hope,
but in this place the healing fingers
are singed and black.

Send them all the beggar,
the ulcerated Lazarus, risen, alive.
Send.
Keep sending.
Your ghost cry may tremble their sleep,
but no words oil the frozen hinge
in the soul.

The Marriage of the King's Son

*He said to his slaves, "The wedding is ready, but those who
were invited were not worthy. Go therefore to the main high-
ways, and as many as you find there, invite to the wedding
feast." (Matthew 22:8-9)*

1

He's working a field.
The fire ants have not come today.
The tomatoes are hard, like calluses
beneath his grip. The leaves are splotched
with flecks of white. His palms itch.

A man appears, slips him an envelope,
walks away.

The fieldworker tears the crease, asks
a friend to read. An invitation to a feast.
A king's feast.
He asks simply, "How can it be?"

You say: Does he go?
The journey is many hours
and costly, even by bus.

2

He sits at a walnut desk,
stares out over the winds and rolls of
his father's empire. He checks the figures,
drums on a drawer leaf, twists the stereo dials.

A man appears, slips him an envelope,
walks away.

He slides the envelope through the electric
opener, reads the invitation, puts it on
the "out" pile, checks his calendar.

As he bends to his work, his eyes stray
back to it again and again.
His mind ambles through a ream of lies.

You say: Does he go?
It's only an hour away by the business Learjet.
His calendar's open.

3
The envelope is on your desk.
The invitation to the feast of the Lamb,
who died for sins and now lives.

Feel the gold lettering.
Sniff the paper.
Let your mind wonder.

You answer: Will you go?
Or find a reasonable reason
to let eternity fly by?

15
The King's Proposal

A great king ruled over a land populated by masses of foolish, sinful, and ungrateful people. They were foolish because they whiled away their days in useless pursuits, spending most of their time searching for entertainment. They were sinful because they disobeyed the king at every turn and were proud of it. And they were ungrateful, which is the usual result of being foolish and sinful.

But the king was something of an entrepreneur. He decided that all wasn't lost. If you had raw material to work with, even if it was rather shoddy at the start, a wise person could always turn an unproductive operation into something profitable. So he set about turning his bankrupt kingdom into one that would run the Dow Jones off the ticker tape.

The first thing he did was provide a way for the average Moe to be adopted into his family. The king decided that personal exposure to himself would benefit all his subjects. Maybe his kingly character would rub off in the process.

But the king knew that merely turning prigs and punks into princes wasn't enough. A punk is still a punk even when he is dressed up in an embroidered tunic and leather shoes. Furthermore, the king didn't want all the new members of his family lying around the palace sipping sassafras tea, shouting, "Servant, Servant," and getting into further trouble with creditors. Thus, he devised an elaborate system of rewards for work well done.

Actually, it wasn't so elaborate. He simply would give crowns (not just one but many) to everyone who performed any service (large or small) that produced lasting results in his kingdom. Good results, that is. He said, "Go to it, my princes, and let's see what you can do."

Well. You'd think they would have been hopping, skipping, and jumping into the fray. But frankly, the princes didn't do a thing. They only took another gulp of sassafras tea, yelled, "Servant," and gazed around at one another to see who would go first. No one moved.

The king might have been stumped. But this was precisely what he'd expected. He called a great convention of all the princes and princesses. He stood before them and said, "My children, we are going to march out and fight dragons."

A groan went up from the gathering, and some even cowered.

"Not the kinds of dragons you'd think—not big ones with whipping tales, monster mouths, and teeth eight inches long. No, we're going after another type. The kind we're going to fight are ten thousand times bigger than any one of us, their tails are known to wipe away whole galaxies at a time, and when they eat, they consume bowls of princes like breakfast cereal."

Now the princes (and princesses) were aghast. Some even murmured (for the first time).

The king held up his hand. "Don't worry," he said. "First of all, I'm providing you with the perfect equipment and tools for slaying such dragons. My tools are infallible, and in the right hands there is no way you can lose. It's only a matter of dropping the carcass. Victory has already been secured."

Now the princes were smiling weakly, and even the princesses raised their eyebrows. But no one was enthusiastic.

"Furthermore," said the king, "my own armies will back you up every step of the way."

Everyone knew the king had the greatest and the best in his armies and that they'd never been defeated.

"In addition," said the king, "I'm going to give you my battle plan in this book. If you're ever mystified or confused,

126

simply consult the book, and you'll have the answer to dispatching the dragon."

Everyone was quite interested at this point. But it did sound a bit idealistic. One of the princes asked, "Sir, what if while we're looking in the book, the dragon impales us on a tooth?"

"Yeah!" said the other princes and princesses.

The king smiled. "I've taken care of that. For those who will use my book consistently, I'll always provide them with the time they need to consult it. No dragon can attack while you're studying strategy."

Everyone was quite astonished. Another prince raised his hand. "Sir, I know it sounds good, but I'm not skilled with a lance or sword. I fear that I'll be eaten before I can whirl my blade."

Again the king smiled and said, "A good question. I have also provided all that's necessary. Each one of you shall have a squire to accompany you into all battles. He will not only instruct you, but I've also given him special abilities to teach you. He will even empower you to wield your weapons well."

Now the whole crowd was murmuring with happiness, but the king held up his hand again. "Finally, I myself shall be with you in every struggle. You won't see me, but I assure you I'll be there."

"How will we know?" asked another prince.

"Because I'm putting my mark on your hearts. All you'll have to do is look within yourself, and you'll find my mark and know that I am with you."

Everyone began nodding with joy. "What then are we waiting for?" shouted one prince. "Shouldn't we get to it?"

"One other thing," said the king. "For all who go out and slay dragons—big or small, fierce or flaky—I'll give them treasure, crowns, and multiple rewards in my kingdom."

Now everyone was quite astonished.

However, one prince, known to be a bit less foolish than most others, raised his hand. "Pardon me, sir, but I have a question."

"Yes?"

"You're telling us that you'll provide the weapons, outfit us, give us the battle plan, provide a squire to meet all our needs, and that you yourself will go with us into every battle— correct?"

The king nodded.

"And if we use all these things, you promise to give us a reward beyond anything we can imagine?"

"Absolutely. So what is your problem?"

The prince squinted. "I don't get it. You're doing virtually everything for us. All we have to do is go. And yet, you're going to give us unimaginable rewards just for doing that?"

The king smiled. "I guess you could say it that way."

The prince laughed. "Why, it's impossible! We'll be paid more than we'd ever deserve. It's like a businessman who finances the whole operation, does most of the work, then gives his employees the biggest dividends."

The king laughed. "I suppose that's true. I hadn't quite thought of it that way."

The prince then said, "Why are you doing this? Why are you being so generous?"

The king gazed at all the princes and princesses gathered for a long time. It seemed that his kind and loving eyes met everyone's for at least a moment. The whole crowd strained to hear whatever he might say.

"You have asked an important question, my prince. I will give you three answers. First, I'm doing this because I like to be generous. Second, I'm doing it because I have a lot to be generous with."

He paused. No one said a word, until the same prince said, "And what is the third reason?"

"Because," said the king, "I love you."

The princes and princesses were silent. Some just gazed at their king in wonder. Others wept. But gradually a rustle, then a rumble, and finally a joyous hurrah shot through the crowd. Soon all were cheering and lauding the king with shouts and praises.

When it was all over, though, a change came upon all of them and they bowed. All decided that foolishness, sin, and ingratitude were not the way to respond to him. Someone murmured, and soon all were saying, "You are worthy, O King, to receive glory and honor. We will serve you now and forever."

The king smiled, and his eyes misted slightly.

Suddenly, a prince shouted, "To the dragons!" Everyone rushed for the door.

16
The Worst Cases

The meeting was going as usual. The Father was asking where each one had been. What he had learned. What he'd been doing.

Satan hadn't spoken yet. No one knew what subject he'd bring up this time, but it was sure to be unnerving. Why the Father put up with Satan's insistent tirades and taunts no one could explain. Why He even let Satan speak astonished everyone. He always insulted Him terribly. Or raised some impossible question or scenario.

Last time it had been this Job situation. Satan wanted to test Job, prove that his faith and love for the Father was plain selfishness.

Well, that had come out all right. Job had conducted himself worthily and had rebuffed Satan on all fronts. But sooner or later this ranter would latch on to something that even the Father couldn't contradict. Or so some of us thought.

It was when the Father was questioning Starrhythm about his adventure in Mesopotamia that Satan interrupted. "Why are we always talking about these inconsequentials? Why don't we get to the heart of the matter?"

The Father glanced at Satan, then turned back to Starrhythm. "Excuse Me," He said and turned to Satan. "You'll get your turn. But I will be finished with the others first."

Satan remained quiet through the rest of the meeting. Finally, the Father turned back to him. "So what tidings do you bring from your travels?"

"I not only have tidings but also some interesting exhibits for Your Majesty," Satan said with his usual contempt. He pushed out his chest haughtily, and his jewels shown hideously in the beautiful light. I marveled at how they had changed since his rebellion, but I couldn't pinpoint how or why.

"I've brought back with me three recently deceased members of Earth. I—and they—would be most interested in Your commentary on a certain subject."

"What subject?"

"Justice."

The crowd of angelic beings began to shuffle a little, but most were looking in Satan's direction and gave him their attention.

This was the way Satan liked it. He'd have more of them on his side in no time. Not that he'd be particularly fond of them. But he always wanted greater numbers in his rebellion. Everyone knew he planned to overthrow the Father. Why the Father let him go on was a complete mystery to all of us.

Satan continued. "One of Your reasons for the creation of Earth and its people, as I recall, was to demonstrate Your absolute justice, was it not?"

"Agreed."

"I have some interesting cases that I—we ... " Satan peered around at the group and noted that they were sufficiently aghast. He continued, "We'd like to know what You have to say by way of defense."

The Father motioned to Satan to go on.

"First, I bring before you Shalezer." Satan bit his words precisely, as though he took pleasure in each syllable.

"Shalezer," Satan said with a great clearing of his throat, "was born with this gross deformity, as you can see." Satan whipped a cover off the hump that had been lying at his feet and exposed the man for all to see. His deformity pertained to a certain encrustation of the face and limbs, as well as a twisting of the shoulders and trunk so that he looked more like an ancient gnarled tree than a man. Shalezer was silent but smiled slightly, as he glanced around at what must have appeared to be most imposing circumstances.

"Yes," said Satan, raising his face, contemptuously, "Shalezer, through no fault of his own, was born in this condition. He has lived for sixty-three years, a hopeless beggar and reject. He finally died under a tree in the forest where he lived near Ur. No one even buried him. It decomposed there until I found him and restored him to his former condition."

The Father asked, "What is your question?"

Satan raised his chin imperiously. "How could You allow this injustice? He did nothing wrong. Yet, You have not provided anything for him by way of dignity, life, and joy."

Some in the crowd were indignant, for Satan had many allied to him. But it was not their turn to speak, and they knew the Father's laws about that. Still, it was obvious that many were unsettled. It was a question we'd all asked at one time or another during our forays to the Blue Planet. Though we were always sent there to observe, it often raised more issues than we could answer.

The Father answered after a short silence. "You have two other cases. What are they? I will answer when you've presented your full brief."

Satan smiled slyly and drew off another wrap. A child sat at his feet, about seven years old. In contrast to Shalezer, she was cherubic, as beautiful as an angel.

"This child, Halah by name," said the accuser, "resided in the city of Hob. When the Persian armies swept through on their conquests, they beheaded her mother and father. When the soldiers were departing, she ran into the street crying, and they trampled her under the horses' hooves. No one noticed, except one contemptible sergeant, who laughed. When I found her, I returned her to the condition you see, but obviously, she was dead."

"What is your question?" the Father said evenly.

"How could you allow this little girl to experience such a tragedy? This wasn't justice. This was murder, and You know it. You sat up here on Your throne and did nothing to stop those soldiers."

The faces of some of the angels were set and hard. Angry eyes turned to the Father and burned to hear His reply. I myself was curious, even a bit nervous about it, but I felt sure the Father would answer.

Satan slit his eyes and licked his lips, his tongue flickering like a flame. "Behold, Zeph!"

Satan tore off a third covering. A gasp surged through the crowd. We already knew the man named Zeph. We'd seen his wickedness and come away disturbed, angry, vengeful. Many had wanted to see him die long ago. Now here he was.

After noting that Zeph's face was recognized, Satan went on, "As many know, this man, Zeph, ruled Sog, one of the cities of the East. His wickedness was reported far and wide. He and his men raped the virgins in the lands he conquered, then roasted them before his gods and ate their flesh in worship. Few men attained anything close to the wickedness of Zeph. Yet, You let him live for ninety-three years. You brought no punishment upon him but allowed him to act out his perversions to their fullest."

Satan paused and glanced at the myriads about him. It was now just as he loved it. Himself the center. Himself the focus. All listening to him. All waiting for what he'd say.

His voice rose. "And now, I'd like to know what You have to say about how all this relates to Your justice, our august Father."

A rumble rolled through the crowd, but the Father motioned for silence. Instantly, all eyes turned back to Him. "I'd like to ask a few questions of some of the others present."

Satan nodded.

"Michael!"

A voice immediately cried out from the center of the crowd, "Yes, Lord!"

"You were there at the beginning, observing the events in the Garden, were you not?"

"I was, Lord."

"Then you will recall what I told the first pair of humans would happen if they sinned. What was it?"

"That they would die, Lord."

"What did they do?"

133

"They chose to sin."

"Did I or anyone else force them to make that choice?"

Michael paused and glanced at Satan, then waited a moment. "Satan goaded them and made suggestions, Lord."

"Untrue!" Satan shouted.

"Facts are facts," retorted Michael.

"They did what they wanted," shouted Satan.

"I was getting to that," Michael replied.

"Silence!" the Father said to Satan. "Michael will speak."

"Lord, Satan did goad the first humans and tempted them. But no one forced them to make their decision. It was free."

"Did they understand clearly what would happen if they sinned?"

"Yes, Lord."

"So then you would say that they freely put themselves into the condition the whole race is now in—a world full of death, destruction, and misery?"

Michael nodded, and I felt my own eyes jump wide with surprise. Yes, that was true. The human race had knowingly put themselves at the mercy of death, evil, and sin. The Father had warned them, taught them, given them all the tools they needed to win in any test or temptation. So they were reaping the result of their own sin—and that was justice.

Many of us shuffled and murmured, some with approval, others with a hiss.

"Gabriel."

Another voice answered from the far left reaches of the crowd, and a circle formed about him so all could see.

"Gabriel, you have made a special study of humans born like Shalezer, correct?"

"Yes, Lord, I have. I've studied men, women, and children from every age up until now."

"What have been your findings?"

"Mainly, Lord, that these folks are little different from all others in the sense that they have the same desires, needs, hopes, and fears. People around them do tend to be harsh and unkind to them, saying that they are in their condition because of sins—their parents' or their own in a so-called previous life or personal sins they've committed—a teaching we know has been promoted by... "

There was a loud hiss from Satan, but Gabriel went on. "By Satan and those aligned with him."

"Lies!" shouted Satan and some others. "We've only given the humans what they wanted."

Gabriel nodded. "That's true to some degree. We've found that Satan doesn't have many alternatives to truth and relies on humans to give him ideas, but... "

There was another commotion, but the Father called for silence. "We're getting off the subject. What were you saying about the treatment people such as Shalezer receive?"

"Well," said Gabriel, "many of them are avoided and scorned. But the wise men and sages we've sent them have made clear that this is no way to treat the poor and disabled."

"And what is the outcome?"

"Not many listen."

"Whose fault is that?"

"Theirs, Lord," Gabriel said, and I noticed that Satan shook his head with anger but remained silent.

"And is it not true," the Father went on, "that one day all who have mistreated people like Shalezer will pay for each of their crimes?"

"Absolutely," said Gabriel. "You've made that completely clear."

There was a long silence while everyone was thinking. Then the Father said, "Littlelight, come forward."

Littlelight was a well-known and decent angel. He was small, but his answers reflected the truth of the Light in all respects.

"How would you explain the acts of cruelty that the humans do to those like Shalezer?"

Littlelight shifted on his feet, "I'm not sure that my explanation is correct, Lord."

"We'll hear it anyway," said the Father.

"According to my own observations, which I've been making since the sin in the Garden, this cruelty and violence is the result of evil in the hearts of the humans and a consequence of their rebellion against You. They refuse to do what's right, even though You've given them much wisdom on the subject of righteousness. In many cases You have judged people who have done such things, but sometimes You choose to let certain ones live for purposes You have not revealed at present."

"What purposes, Littlelight?"

The small angel shifted his weight again, rolled up on his toes slightly, and said, "To offer a simple opinion, Lord, I think it's because such individuals are an example of Your patience and love and Your desire to see them turn back to You. It may also help the other humans learn to trust You and not the things they see happening around them."

I had to nod with respect at Littlelight's answer and resolved to get to know him better. It would be good to compare notes with him on our quest to further understand the Father's ways.

The Father turned back to Satan, but Littlelight continued. "Lord, one other thing. Mostly the humans mistreat one another. But I've observed that . . ." He glanced at Satan, and I saw the archangel tighten and snarl, casting a nasty look at the smaller Littlelight.

But the angel went on, "I've observed that many of those associated with Satan's rebellion have taken liberties with the humans, led them on, and have even caused direct harm themselves."

"Another lie!" shouted Satan. But I could tell some of the air had gone out of his voice. "A vicious lie! If anything was done, it was only to prove a point. We're at war here."

The Father motioned for silence again, and Satan set his jaw, gnashing his teeth. "Shalezer, step forward."

The deformed man unwound himself and stood up.

"You have lived a hard life, haven't you?" The Father's eyes were kind. I even detected pain in his voice.

"I have, Father," said Shalezer, "but I honestly believe You've been good to me, too. I was taught the truth at a young age, and though many hated me, I had friends too—good people, some of whom are down there, still being mistreated. I hope You'll help them stand up to it like You did with me."

"So you were a believer?" said the Father.

"Oh, yes," said Shalezer. "I didn't even want this person—" he motioned to Satan, "to get me involved in this. But he gagged me and . . . "

"False!" yelled Satan, but I could see he was deflated at this new revelation.

Shalezer held up the gag for all to see. "You see, I saved it, Lord. I thought it might come in handy."

Some of the crowd were snickering now, but Satan had extracted a claw and was reaching toward the poor man when Michael yelled, "The Lord rebuke you!"

Instantly, the Father motioned and three guards stepped forward to hold Satan in place. "If you're going to act like this, Archangel, you will be restrained," said the Father.

Satan shook the guards off. "I just want to see justice done."

"Right, like the way you tamper with human genes!" Gabriel said.

Satan screamed again, but the Father turned to Gabriel. "What is this?"

"Shalezer, sir. The reason he's deformed is because one of the rebels pulled some tricks with the genetic code when he was conceived."

There were shouts all over the auditorium, and it looked like a fight might break out. But the Father spoke, and all became quiet. "Enter into the joy of your Father," He said, and instantly the ugly man was transformed into a perfection of humanity and ushered out.

Before we had a chance to react, the Father called Zeph. The evil man stepped forward, rubbing his hands together. He was a huge specimen with scars on neck and cheeks. An obvious strongman.

"I am here."

The Father looked at him with an even glow in His eyes, unlike the way he looked at Shalezer. "Do not be afraid. Only answer truthfully. Is it true that you were a wicked man?"

Zeph sighed and bowed. "It is true."

"Is it also true that before each of the crimes you committed I spoke to you and warned you of the consequences?"

Zeph nodded. "Yes, at one time I had a strong conscience."

137

"And is it true that in spite of the men who counseled you to do evil, I sent several who warned you repeatedly about your wrong behavior?"

The man seemed to shrink in size. "Yes, Lord."

"What did you do to those men?"

"I sacrificed them to my gods as offerings. I hated them."

The whole assembly gasped.

"Who are your gods?"

Zeph gulped and looked at Satan momentarily, who raised a taloned hand, threateningly. But Zeph straightened up and pointed to the Accuser. "Him and others with him."

Satan shouted with rage. "He may have offered those men, but they were unacceptable. We didn't want them."

"Your priests told me you wanted them dead!" shouted Zeph. "I was following their instructions!"

Satan leaped toward the man, but the Father spoke a word, and the Accuser was stopped. Then He said to two angels next to Zeph, "Take him out and confine him."

Then, "Halah, step forward."

The little girl stood, shaking and afraid. But as she looked into the Father's eyes, she seemed to grow in stature and strength. "We understand that you lost your parents and your life to the soldiers of Persia."

"That is true, Father."

"What were your beliefs, child?"

Halah didn't pause. For a seven-year-old, she seemed to know the answer readily. "My parents did not follow the gods of our land, but they told me about a great Creator. Our family has always loved and desired to serve Him."

"Who was that Creator?"

She paused and looked into the Father's eyes. "I think it was You, Father." Her voice was high and beautiful. "Was it?"

"Yes," the Father said.

She bowed momentarily before Him.

The Father went on. "Do you feel that I have wronged you in allowing you to die?"

Halah trembled, but she said, "My father told me that everyone must die one day. Then we go to live with the Creator —You—forever. So I don't see much difference between dying now or when I'm as old as Mother or Father." She paused, thinking. "I still believe You could have stopped the soldiers and let me live longer."

She stopped again and pressed her hand to her chin. "But then I would have been left with no family and our village destroyed. Maybe I would have been sold into slavery, maybe to a horrid Persian."

I was astonished that a seven-year-old could look at things so wisely.

The Father interrupted my thoughts, "So you are saying that you trust My judgment in allowing what happened?"

Halah bowed. "I guess I don't have any other choice." She smiled. "But I think I can do it gladly."

The Father looked back at the crowd and then at Satan, but Halah spoke again. "Can I say something else, Lord?"

The Father nodded.

She bowed again. "I don't understand all this, but will you make this horrid Satan person let me go? He's been a beast. He tells me not to say this and that I should say that, then tells me lies about You and Your kingdom. It's terrible."

Satan screamed and leaped at her, raking at the child's face. A quick word from the Father held him.

"You needn't say any more, Halah," said the Father. "You are released." Immediately, one of the angels took her by the hand and led her away from the crowd.

Finally, the Father fixed on Satan with stern eyes. "Are you satisfied?"

"Not at all!" he shouted. "You haven't proved anything. It's all tricks. There's more to it than this little charade. I have better proofs than these."

"Feel free to bring them in," the Father said.

He looked back at the rest of us as Satan and his group stalked out. Michael said, "Shall we sing now, Lord?"

The Father shook His head. "Alas, it is not yet the time. But soon it will be time, dear Michael."

He looked at the rest of us. For the first time, I noticed the pain in His eyes. I knew this problem of evil must have dragged terribly at His great heart. But I had not known until then how deeply it hurt Him.

Just the same, though, I knew He had a plan. It was un-folding before us. I was eager to get back to the Blue Planet and see some more examples of His mercy, and grace, and justice. But for now, the meeting was over. And I had to get back to my studies.

17

Report on Giving

This is a report from the angelic archives in which Gabriel, well-known angelic messenger in the Bible, reports to Michael, his superior, about his discoveries concerning giving by humans for the sake of God's kingdom. In this case, he has investigated the results of the giving of the widow (in Mark 12:41-44), who put two "mites," or lepta,* into the Temple treasury. Also examines the man in the same incident (who is called Zechariah), purported to be rich (by subhuman standards).

Memo

DATE: Last Days, June 12
TO: MichaEL, Archangel
FR: GabriEL

The accounting records are, as you indicated, superb. I had not realized accounts were so exact—though I should have expected it. I arrived at the recording chamber early.

---

* These sums are difficult to determine in modern dollars. The best way of calculation is to take the drachma (or denarius) as one day's ordinary wages for a laborer. Making that equal to $64, at $8 per hour for a typical day's wages, that would make a lepton equal to 50 cents (1/128 of a denarius). A mina was equal to 100 drachma, or $6400. And a talent equaled 6,000 drachma, or the equivalent of $384,000.

DaniEL was courteous and efficient, as you said. He took me directly to the recording angel to look at the accounts on the widow.

But first he showed me the records for gifts also given on the Monday that the widow gave her two "mites." The ledger reads as follows:

Name	Gift
Zechariah	1 talent (silver), 14 drachma, 6 lepta
Mallagran	23 drachma
Eli	4 minas, 22 drachma, 26 lepta
Mariel	12 drachma, 4 lepta
Matthel	2 minas, 6 drachma
The widow	2 lepta

There was a break in the accounts at this point because of Jesus' comments on what the widow was putting in. He said, "Truly I say to you, this poor widow put in more than all the contributors to the treasury; for they all put in out of their surplus, but she, out of her poverty, put in all she owned, all she had to live on." It was a sound enough statement, but Satan has argued through his lawyer, Zob, that the two mites (or lepta) that the widow put in hardly amounted to anything and could not possibly have counted as much as the others. The Lord has told Satan to wait until the end for the final accounting on that issue. I'm sure Jesus' words will be vindicated.

But also, because of the commotion around the widow, Satan claimed that three of his disciples in the line were overlooked. However, I found the records quite exact.
Those three were:

Malchi	3 minas, 22 drachma, 2 lepta
Abel	16 drachma, 2 lepta
Canel	1 mina, 12 drachma, 2 lepta

Zob argued that each of these three put in two lepta, the same as the widow, and that Jesus should have given them similar recognition. But this was clearly a case of devilogic and missed the point, so it was thrown out of the throne room.

142

The more interesting scenario is that of the results of the widow's two cents (actually, quarter cents). What came of the money she donated? Certainly, from a purely economic point of view, it appears that her gift was far less than any of the others. But as we know, the Lord does not work on the basis of pure economics. His kingdom is spiritually based. Thus, I pursued the issue and discovered the following:

The widow's gift was credited against a certain scribe's work (Ezekijah) in the copy room. The Lord used the two lepta to pay for the scribe's time while he copied a portion of the prophet Isaiah from a worn scroll to a new one. To be exact, the money was accounted as paying for the scribe's work from 2:46 to 2:49 in the afternoon on June 13 of that year. In that time slot, he copied from the old scroll the verses we know as Isaiah 53:4-6, which says, "Surely our griefs He Himself bore, and our sorrows He carried; yet we ourselves esteemed Him stricken, smitten of God, and afflicted. But He was pierced through for our transgressions, He was crushed for our iniquities; the chastening for our well-being fell upon Him, and by His scourging we are healed. All of us like sheep have gone astray, each of us has turned to his own way; but the Lord has caused the iniquity of us all to fall on Him."

(The Temple, of course, records the widow's lepta as going into a fund to replace gold on the ceilings, and the actual pieces were used in an illegal moneychanging transaction ending up in the hands of a Pharisee, Zepheli. But that has little to do with divine accounting, as we know. God does not work as men.)

But back to the scroll. This new scroll remained in the Temple for several years. Many of the apostles read from this portion and used it to prove Jesus was the Messiah. Several thousand lost ones (4,322, by angelic reckoning) were reclaimed during this period. The apostle Paul himself used the passage frequently. He had a direct effect on some 36,755 people (up until his beheading). Only omniscience can bring it all together statistically, though, of course, that is the least of our concerns.

I found that Peter read from Isaiah 53 several times that year in answer to objections from Pharisees. In one case, for instance, a young man named David ben Matthew was listening. He was a learned Jew, though young, and believed Jesus had not been the Messiah.

However, upon hearing Peter's exposition of the words in Isaiah 53—to be precise, verse six—that man's iniquities were laid on Him; this David's heart was pricked. The Spirit spoke to him, and he became a believer at that moment.

What does all this have to do with the widow?

First, it was her lepta that paid for those words to be written, as I've said.

But second, the way our Lord does His accounting involves a rather important process of "royalties." That is, any *effects* of a gift originally given to be used in faith are as much a part of the deed as the gift itself. Thus, effects on people from that particular passage thereafter go to the widow's account (and to anyone else involved—I found that the widow herself had been given one lepta by an old man of faith, so he profits too).

Anyway, the fact is that every time those verses are read by Peter or anyone else, the kingdom effects all go to the widow's account! Frankly, MichaEL, I found myself wishing I were that widow! But there's more.

Beyond all this is the fact that this scroll went on to become the standard on which many of the later scrolls were based. We record that some 433,622,565 people have been influenced by that text from that day to the present hour (A.D. 1990), but those figures change every moment.

By way of angelic interest stories (there are so many, but I chose these two), let me relate the following facts. You will recall an episode in which one of our angelren instructed Philip to walk down a road toward Gaza. (You will find the exact reference in Acts 8:26-40; how I wish Luke had been able to tell more about it.)

Philip met an Ethiopian, a eunuch and official of the high court of Candace, queen of the Ethiopians. This man was reading from a text of Isaiah, and Philip asked him if he understood it. He didn't, so Philip explained the text, directed him to Jesus, and baptized him.

What text was the Ethiopian reading? The one the widow's lepta was used to copy! I'm still investigating how the Master engineered this. For now, I'll file it under "Unsearchable Wisdom."

More important, this eunuch went back to his kingdom a Christian. He spoke to Candace of his newfound faith, led several in her court to Him, and eventually went on to become a powerful evangelist in that land. To this day, the church he began there still survives.

All this—all those souls, all that good, everything that happened to advance the kingdom of the Lord Himself—will go to the widow's account too. When she gets to heaven, she'll be one of the richest folks there—no doubt about it! That is, if there could be such comparisons in heaven.

The second episode occurred around A.D. 1548. A young mother received an inheritance. Not a great sum, but it would have put her family in scarlet. Shortly thereafter, a plague struck the city, and many were without food and clothing. She wondered what she might do and decided, on the basis of the widow's story in Scripture, to use it to start a small bread, meat, and stocking ministry to the needy. She called it "The Widow's Purse." This woman turned out to be Martin Luther's wife. (Not that it should make any difference.) She continued to influence others as well as her husband to help needy people on the basis of the widow's gift. (Incidentally, I've noted some 16,024 individual works performed on the basis of the widow's story all over the world.)

MichaEL, the stories go on and on ad infinitum. (Not literally, of course. We know there are very exact figures here, but having been down among so many people of late, I'm learning a few of their odder expressions.) It's most gratifying to see what the Lord can do with two lepta.

The alarming thing I note in all this is what the widow hoped would happen with her lepta. As usual, I find humans —even the faithful—thinking in the sparest of terms. Her thought was only that her lepta might buy a brick for the Temple wall. Little did she know it would become a foundation sapphire in the New Jerusalem!

Next study: What does He do with a whole life of lepta, good deeds, kind words, prayers?

Note

GabriEL: What were your findings on Zechariah?

MichaEL

Memo

TO: MichaEL
FR: GabriEL

Sorry to have failed to mention Zechariah. As you know, he donated more than a talent of silver, which is an awesome sum. I didn't try to account for the exact figures—let's just say it amounts to thousands of days' wages. He wanted his gift used to purchase pillars in the main alcove of the Temple. This was precisely what he got. It purchased two pillars. He had gold plates with his name on them affixed to the pillars. They stood for some forty years and were admired by many.

But as you know, a pillar (being somewhat immovable) doesn't do much to advance the kingdom of God, nor does it have verbal power to convert those who look at it. (He didn't affix a sign to the pillar to tell people about the gospel or anything; only his name was prominent.)

The Temple, as you know, was destroyed in A.D. 70. Only the Master really knows what happened to the pillars, but records say the pieces went into a Roman roadbed, and the gold was discovered to be brass and junked. (He was cheated by a Sadducee.)

As far as any rewards Zechariah would have received (had he converted), there is no telling. I don't care to investigate possibilities. But thanks for prodding my curiosity.

18
Grandfather's Key

Grandfather lay dying on the roughly hewn oak bed. The family gathered hurriedly to hear his last words. After speaking to many of those standing about him, he turned to Philip, aged sixteen.

"These, my son, are the keys that open the treasuries of the king. They have been passed on from your ancestors and now to you. You must journey to the king's palace in Sunn Almann, the same journey I took ages ago. He will show you all you could ever desire to see."

He handed them to Philip, but their unexpected weight made them fall through his hands. "They're so heavy, Grandfather," he said. "I can't lift them."

"Yes, but they'll grow lighter as you learn to wear them. All my days I wore them over my heart. You will wear them, too."

When Grandfather had distributed his possessions among the clan weeping about him, he gave a final blessing and breathed his last.

A cry of lament went up, but Philip inched out dragging the keys. Outside in the sunlight he touched them and felt their remarkable heat. There were two keys, each with interesting insignia on the round part at the top. One pictured a man who appeared to be in agony, and the other was an open book. With a tear in his eye, Philip turned and gave his grandfather a final salute.

As he grew, Philip thought often of the trip to Sunn Al-mann. He practiced lifting the keys, and eventually, he was able to wear them around his neck easily. He grew strong as he wore them daily, and a gentle, transforming power came over him that gave him a clear mind, a steadfast heart, and pure eyes.

When he reached twenty-one years, his father told him it was time for the journey. In a short time, he was packed and ready. At the gate, he kissed his parents, sisters, and brothers and set off amid their cheers and shouts of encouragement.

After many hours he met an old man traveling in the same direction. The man begged company, and soon they were traveling together. He asked Philip where he was going. Philip told him about the keys. The old man was incredulous. "Do you believe that fairy tale?" he challenged.

Philip stopped, his mouth open. "I never thought not to believe it."

The old man snorted. "You don't think the king would allow you into his treasury, do you? You're just a peasant. He's a king. What kind of person do you think he is?"

Suddenly, Philip was filled with doubt. But as he peered at the old man and reflected on his grandfather and his last words, the heaviness departed. "My choice, then, is whether to believe you or my grandfather. I'll go with my grandfather, thank you."

The old man muttered something about a stone in his shoe and stopped, waving the lad on.

Several days later, Philip came to a fork in the road. No sign directed him, and he wasn't sure which way to go. A youth lolled on the grass in the middle, so Philip asked, "Which way to Sunn Almann?"

The youth lazily waved toward the rocky path to the right. "Why are you headed there?" he asked.

Philip sat down and spun out his tale.

The youth only chuckled. "I know of far better places, easier to get to and with more treasure."

Philip raised his eyebrows. "You've been to Sunn Almann?"

148

"No," said the youth. "But I've been to the other places. And everyone there scorns Sunn Almann."

"So how do you know the other places are better?"

"Look at me," he said and stood up. To be sure, he was finely dressed, with a golden sword and scabbard. "Down the road just a few miles is Carn Valley. There, you turn in your keys, and they'll give you a time like you've never had before. I did it years ago, and I've never regretted it. Everything's free."

"Just for the keys?" asked Philip.

The youth hedged a bit, saying, "Well, there's a bit more involved, but it's a lot easier than walking all the way to Sunn Almann for treasure you haven't even seen. Give them to me now, and I'll take you there."

Philip jumped back. "And why should I take Carn Valley's treasures over those of the king?"

The youth laughed. "You can choose either way. But only those who love sweat, hardship, and work go to Sunn Almann."

Philip shook his head. "No, if it was good enough for Grandfather, it's good enough for me. I think I'll head my own way."

The youth shrugged, and Philip hopped up and began climbing the steep road. It was wearisome work, but when he reached a house on the side of the hill, an old man offered him a drink.

"Headed for Sunn Almann, I expect?" he said.

"Yes," said Philip wearily. "You've been there?"

"No," he said with a knowing smile. "I suppose you've got some keys."

Philip nodded.

"I have a set myself," he said. "My grandfather gave them to me. But I have been poking around here for years. Just too much uphill work, I guess. I have the keys in the house. Want to see them?"

Philip backed out of the yard. He didn't like the man's demeanor, and he said, "No, sir. I've really got to keep going. But thanks for the drink."

He walked off without looking back. "Why don't any of these people take the keys seriously?" he muttered, but he could think of no answer.

After many days of steep ascending and descending, Philip spied the king's palace. It shone in the sun the same way the keys did. When he reached the door, he knocked briskly and waited. An ancient man answered.

"I've come to see the king," said Philip, when the man asked him his business.

"I'm the king," said the man, smiling.

Philip was astonished but bowed deeply.

The king said, "I don't look like what you expected?"

Philip shook his head, hesitantly.

The king chuckled. "Everyone finds me different than they imagined. It's part of being a king. I assume you have some keys."

Philip showed him the keys and entered the large front room.

"Tomorrow," said the king, "we'll see to your treasures."

The next morning they had a fine breakfast. Finally, the king showed him a door. "There are four doors. You must match the key to the door and then insert and open it."

Philip looked at his keys. "But I only have two keys."

The king smiled. "You will find the others along the way."

The first door Philip came to was small and tarnished. As Philip gazed at it, it seemed that he saw the face of a man in pain in its gold leaf. Immediately, he matched the key with the face of a man on it and put it in the slot. It twisted easily.

When the door opened, he was thrust out upon a long ledge with a narrow walk to the next door. He trembled as he walked across, then read the inscription on the door: "Life is more than words, but it's the Word that gives the life."

Philip examined his keys once again and matched the key with the book etched onto its surface. He tried it, and the door opened.

This time the door opened onto a small lawn that surrounded a pool of water. Philip looked around but saw no door. Coming closer to the pool of water, he read these words

150

etched into the grass: "The key to this door lies in your mind; see it there, and you will never be left behind."

Philip wondered at the words and reasoned that if the pool was the door, somehow he must produce the key with his mind. He began to imagine a key and a slot in the water. As he pictured himself inserting the key into the slot, he turned it, and suddenly there was a click. The lawn and pool disappeared, and he was plunged into darkness.

At first he could see nothing. The darkness was tangible and seemed as heavy as a curtain. But as he peered about, he glimpsed a lone torch burning far away. He walked toward it. When he reached it, he saw the fourth door next to it in the air. It was a monstrous blank space of black. There was no place for a key and no hint of what to do.

When he looked at the torch, he marveled as the flames began dancing and spelling out another inscription. "The Spirit gives light, and with it the darkness is exposed and thrust back."

Philip decided that the torch itself might be the key. He took it from its holder and thrust it into the dark space that was the door. Instantly, the darkness shrank back. But the light that appeared was so blinding, he winced and closed his eyes. "Ow!" he cried.

Gradually, he tried to open his eyes, and as he slit them, the light became bearable. In a moment, he was gazing in wonder. He stood in the middle of myriads of treasures. They stretched before him, jumbled together from horizon to horizon in a multitude of shapes and forms. To his left were chests shining heavy with golden chips. To his right, a box played gentle strains of music, which, when Philip listened, filled his heart and made him want to shout. Behind him was a table laden with food whose odors didn't affect his nose as much as his brain; as he sniffed, he seemed to see farther and deeper into himself and into the things about him. Immediately before him was a cage in which a small bird sang. The song touched him and filled him with a wonderful calm he'd never known before. Beyond all these were more and greater treasures.

Suddenly, the king was at his side. "You have found your way well. Shall we begin to examine the treasures?"

Philip gulped. "Maybe we should just look at the ones for me."

The king smiled. "They're all for you."

He blinked and stared again at the landscape shimmering in the light. "How could I take it all away?" he asked.

"How big is your heart?" asked the king.

Philip looked at him quizzically.

"All these will fit into your own heart. The only thing that restricts the amount of treasure a man can claim is the size of his heart."

Philip gazed about him again in amazement. The king said, "You'll understand these things as you go along. Where would you like to begin?"

He looked at the cage with the bird singing inside. "Here."

19
The True Music

The town of Magic Prairie had lost the True Music.

Many years ago they had been a happy people. Great oaks lined their humblest streets. Children played happily in the yards. And they all had the True Music. Whenever you met someone from Magic Prairie, he or she sang. Robustly. Earnestly. With penetrating lyric and uplifting tune.

The music had the power to unite souls and transform them inside out—it was the True Music. You wanted to laugh and cry, dance, shout, and sit quietly gazing across the snowy fields all at once. Everyone said it was the most peaceful, joyful, beautiful music they'd ever heard.

You could read about it in the great books. The people were empowered. They danced. Peace reigned. Disputes were settled and lives knit together in harmonies of happiness.

And now it was gone.

How? Somehow, the music had been lost, forgotten. It was stolen or hidden away or just overlooked. But no one remembered the True Music anymore, what lyric it spoke, or what tune it set. Not old Abraham. Not ancient Missie Lee. Not the children of Lincoln Avenue. No one.

Sometimes the old folks spoke of it quietly and wistfully. But no one could so much as hum a bar of it, let alone the whole tune. In fact, many were saying that the True Music never existed. It was a myth of the past. A legend. "You know the old ones," said the mayor. "Superstitious. We simply should set our minds at ease and not worry about it."

But many did worry. Since the True Music had gone out of their lives, the young ones had grown up mean. Crime flourished. Years earlier, no one had locked a front door or a back door. But now the barns and even the outhouses were locked. No one trusted anyone else. There was little love. Most of all, there was no joy or peace at Christmas or Easter or during the summer songfests. People spent their days and nights complaining about everything.

One evening, a few of the people of Magic Prairie got together to talk about the situation. After much discussion, they decided that someone should travel over the mountains to the Keeper of the True Music's castle. It was called "The Many Rooms of Music," and it contained all the music of the world, including the True Music.

Someone would have to go, get the True Music, and bring it back to Magic Prairie.

After much argument, David the Younger stepped forward to say that he and his two brothers, Samuel and Joshua, would make the arduous journey. But, they asked, "How will we know the True Music when we hear it? The castle is said to have many, many rooms of music."

They discussed the problem late into the night. Someone said the True Music made you want to dance and sit still all at once. But another objected that that wasn't logical. The priest said, "You'll just know, that's all."

"But how?" David asked, vehemently. He and his brothers didn't want to make a journey without some idea of what they were looking for.

"When it happens, you just know," the priest said with a shrug, but even he had no idea.

David wasn't satisfied. "There has to be a way to recognize the True Music. We can't claim it unless we know what it sounds like."

A few others suggested that the three brothers try some of the old songs. However, they already knew the old songs, and everyone said, "They were all without joy." In fact, no one was able to sing one correctly. People argued with one another when they were sung, and there were often many different versions of the same song.

Finally, one of the older men stood up and said, "Let us cry out to the Keeper of the True Music and ask his help."

"No one knows who the Keeper is," the mayor said. But everyone agreed it was worth a try. David and his brothers closed their eyes and cried out to the Keeper of the True Music to guide them.

The next day the three brothers set off on their search. Their departure was a gala occasion. Many women turned out with goodies for the trip. Had they taken all of them, they would have needed a wagon. But one lass gave each of them a fine cheesecake, and they packed one in each knapsack. Then with many slaps on the back, the three set off.

On the way, each meditated on what the True Music might sound like. Their minds filled with questions, and they had no answers. Hour after hour on the road they would stop and call out to the Keeper to give them wisdom.

At last, after many days they reached the road to the castle of the Many Rooms of Music. David, Samuel, and Joshua felt frightened and sick at heart. "What are we to do?" they asked each other repeatedly. They continued to stop and cry out to the Keeper of the True Music to help them. But no help seemed to come. David told his brothers to have faith, but they were all very much afraid.

On the final stretch of road up to the castle, they met an old man with a flowing white beard. He sat alone by the road, strumming a little guitar. He was bald, with fiery eyes. At his feet lay a staff.

Since it was lunchtime, the three brothers stopped to talk and share what was left of their cheesecake with him. A stream burbled nearby, and each brother swilled a long drink from it. The old man asked David to fill his jug, and David did so.

The old man played many songs on his guitar, and each had a beauty that the brothers thought might be like the True Music. Finally, Samuel said, "Kind sir, do you know anything about the True Music?"

The old man smiled. He strummed his guitar and played a strange tune with even stranger words.

The True Music comes quiet and loud,
It speaks to the heart; it comes with a cloud.
It takes what you are; it teaches you truth.
It gives young men wisdom and gives old men youth.
It takes what you are; it makes your song soar.
It takes who you are and makes you more.

"What does it mean?" asked David.

The old man said, "I will give you each a song. The test of the True Music is this: When the three songs dance together, when you feel wise in its grip, when you are yourself and more, then you will have found the True Music."

He sang a song that David learned easily. Then he gave one to Samuel and another to Joshua. Each song was different in tune, rhyme, and pace. When they sang them together, they clashed. The three boys were mystified. The young men sang their songs to themselves as they walked with the old man, but they could do nothing to make them work together.

"Are these the only songs we should sing?" asked Joshua, who was often creative.

"Ah, you will learn the secret of the True Music when the three songs dance," said the old man.

As he spoke, they came to a fork in the road, and he told them he had to take the low road into town but the high road went to the castle. They parted with thanks.

David and each of his brothers whistled the tunes as they headed up the road. A glimmer of joy broke across each boy's soul, but nothing more. They were just ordinary songs like those they had learned in Magic Prairie.

Before long, they arrived at the castle of the Many Rooms of Music. A guard let them in and told them they could go into as many rooms as they liked. Others at the door were given similar instructions. Some had come looking for the True Music, whereas others sought music of other sorts. Still others were only curious. Some seemed to have been forced to come, representing their towns and villages and saying they simply wanted to get it over with and get back to their places of business.

156

David, Samuel, and Joshua walked through the castle, and peered at many doors with inscriptions on them in strange writing. People would go through a door and disappear for some time, then come out. Sometimes they looked happy when they went in and unhappy when they came out. Some came out singing. Others just went in and came out, only to head for another room. The three brothers decided to try a tall bronze door with a woman pictured on it.

There was a crowd of people inside, and they listened to a woman singing marvelously on a couch. She seemed to be unaware of the group. Every now and then, she'd break into a loud, raucous laugh. This usually happened when someone in the crowd began singing the song with her or some other song. At that moment, she'd look at them, pick out the person singing, wink at him, and send him out, saying, "Sing the song, friend. Take it to your people and sing." The person would then depart, often with a laugh and a shout.

David remembered the tune the old man gave him and began to whistle it. As he did, he drew nearer to the woman.

Immediately, she began singing all the louder.

He tried to hear himself above her singing, but her music swallowed up his tune. He couldn't hear anything but her song—and he didn't like it. As his brothers tried to sing, they found that they were all soon absorbed and overcome by the woman's song.

"She just drowns us out," David said to them, and they headed for the door. When they opened it, they heard the woman laugh her raucous, vile laugh again.

The three brothers came to another door with strange letters on it. Since there were only a few people inside, they went in.

A little elf sat on a couch. He had wrinkled jowls, and a kind, sunburned face. The moment they stepped up to observe, the elf pointed them out. "Sing your tunes," he said.

David and his brothers each began to whistle. As they did, the elf produced a baton and began giving directions. "A little louder," he whispered to Samuel. "Slower, you," he said to Joshua. And, "Quietly now," he whispered to David.

The three young men worked at doing as the elf said, thinking that perhaps this was the True Music, for their songs always seemed at the point of merging and even dancing. But as he jumped around, getting each person in the room to sing, the room was soon jumping with such a cacophony that nothing made any sense.

"Now hit that high note with a bit of volume," the elf shouted to one.

"Tone down over there," he yelled to another.

"Now staccato, some staccato there," the elf bellowed to a big man.

Then, "Quickly, now. Now slow, like a mule."

The elf went on and on. Nothing made any sense. The three brothers only felt tired. Their mouths were dry, the music bored them, and the directions became more difficult to follow.

"Up, up!" yelled the elf. "Now down, way down."

The three brothers finally turned away in disgust. "We can't reach those notes," they said.

"Too bad," said the elf. "We were doing so well. Next."

"But it doesn't make any sense," said Samuel.

The elf shrugged. "Who said it was supposed to make sense?"

They went on down the hall to a door that said, "Music of the Howling Dog." It sounded strange enough, so they went in.

A dog sat on the floor, whimpering and slobbering. The three boys watched. The dog made no other sounds, so David decided to whistle his tune just to see what might happen.

Instantly, the dog picked the tune up. It began howling the tune, exactly as David whistled it. David sang a bar, the dog sang a bar. It was a marvelous duet.

Then Samuel joined in. And Joshua.

Somehow the dog managed to howl every one of the tunes at once. It was almost funny. Then they noticed something. The dog began to change the tunes with his own words and melodies. The three brothers couldn't keep on track.

Soon the dog had taken over their tunes completely, and they were all howling in unison with him. They went faster

158

and faster. In a minute, they howled nothing but deep, guttural, dog sounds.

The three brothers ran for the door. Once out, they leaned against a wall, breathing hard. "I've forgotten the tune completely," cried Samuel.

So had David and Joshua. Each brother tried to sing their music several ways, but the tunes had fled their minds.

"What has happened?" cried David.

No one knew. "Cry to the Keeper of the True Music," said Joshua. "Maybe he'll help us remember."

They all cried out to the Keeper, and as they calmed down, their minds cleared, and the song of the howling dog released its grip on them. Each remembered the tune the old man had given them.

"We must be more careful in the next room," Samuel said.

They went through thirty or forty more rooms, each with different and strange kinds of music. After a long while they came to a small door with no inscription, just an A and a Z emblazoned on it.

When they opened the door, a fresh blast of air struck their tired faces. Each felt stronger, and they pushed their way in.

Once in, the wind calmed down. It blew all around them, quiet and serene. It felt pleasant on the face and lips. David stood by the wall and listened, while Samuel and Joshua sat down. "At least we can rest here for a few minutes. It's nice," said Samuel.

They lay back and let the air roll over them.

No sound but the wind came to them. In a few moments, they all felt sleepy. As he drifted off, David began to sing his song.

Immediately, the wind picked up the tune. At first, there were no real sounds, just a deep, mournful murmur through the room. But the tune seemed to fit the murmur, and the murmur the tune.

David stood up with a start. He stopped whistling, but the wind did not stop. It had picked up the tune, and was doing wonderful things with it. The melody was the same, but the wind had added harmony. There was new depth, and the tune had a greater beauty.

"Samuel," David called, "sing."

Samuel sat up and sang his tune. The moment he did, the wind blew all around it until it began to mix David and Samuel's tune in a wondrous duet.

"How did it do that?" David cried. He leaped and kicked his heels together. "I feel like dancing."

Samuel shouted, "Joshua, sing your song."

Joshua added his own tune to what the wind was doing with the other two songs. Instantly, the wind echoed the tune, adding new melodies and harmonies. All three young men sang their songs, but the wind seemed to take each and mingle it beautifully, like the weaving of a great tapestry. One moment, David's words were emphasized, then Samuel's, and finally Joshua's. The three boys felt lighter than air and swayed and danced to the music.

Soon, several more people entered and began whistling as well, but their tunes were all different. Still, the wind picked up all the tunes, each one different and beautiful, and wove them together into a fine piece. They sang together with a radiance and life that the tunes, when sung alone, lacked.

"The True Music," David whispered, and Samuel and Joshua agreed.

They sang for hours. No one tired. Sometimes the wind leaped and soared. At times lightning flashed, and there was a great roll of thunder. Sometimes a cloud seemed to form over them and undulate to the sound of the music, as though watching. But it all worked together, like a marvelous symphonic work. Sometimes one or two of those present found their tune magnified and shaped, while the others sank back, providing background and harmony.

A deep contentment came over David and his brothers. Their hearts danced. They remembered the old man's words: "When the tune begins to dance." Now they were sure.

Finally, the wind quieted and returned to its normal blowing, and the group went out the door. There was much joking and merriment, and everyone told each other where they were from so they could visit one another in the future.

When the others had departed, David suddenly said, "How do we take the True Music with us?"

Samuel and Joshua glanced at one another. They didn't know.

David bowed his head. "Let's ask the Keeper of the True Music to show us." They prayed together.

David looked up. "Maybe I should sing." He began singing his song.

Instantly, the wind that had been in the room was about them, in his heart and mouth and molding the tune into something beautiful. Samuel and Joshua sang with him, and the same thing happened.

"Then we can take it with us," exulted David. They set off down the road singing their songs.

When they reached Magic Prairie, they told the people their story. The three boys began singing their songs, the wind blew, and the True Music resounded through the hills.

"Teach us," cried the people, and each of the boys taught a group the song he had learned.

Soon, the whole village was singing a wondrous symphony of True Music. It was marvelous. They danced and sang under the sun with lightness in their feet and hearts.

As they sang, a little girl walked up and began singing a song she'd learned in school. Everyone stopped. Someone was about to scold her, as it wasn't one of the songs the three brothers had taught them, but the wind took her song and added it to the others, mixing it and weaving it beautifully with what was already being sung.

An old man stood up. "Maybe I can sing a favorite song of mine that I learned years ago. Maybe it will work, too."

"Try it!" said David.

The old man sang. Again, the wind caught it.

"Perhaps I can sing something I myself composed," said another young man, a friend of the three brothers.

"Sing it," everyone shouted.

He did, and the wind caught and carried it up to heaven with the others.

"What is this then?" said the priest. "Whatever we sing, the wind catches and mingles with the True Music. Is there no True Music?"

No one knew what to say.

Then Joshua spoke. "Remember what the old man said: When the three songs dance, and when each of you remains himself and yet becomes more than himself—then you will have found the True Music."

David cried out. "I know now. The True Music happens when the Keeper of the Music mixes his own music with the music of our hearts. It's the heart that matters, not the music."

Everyone became silent, and the wind murmured in the background. "We should thank the Keeper of the True Music for uniting us again," said Samuel. They prayed, and as they spoke the wind took their prayer, mingled it in song, and soon every heart was filled with the true music.

20

The Man Who Wanted a Little Bit of Everything

Ralph Pyle was a busy guy. He didn't want much. He didn't expect a lot. Not the moon or the stars or a home in Malibu. But he did want a little bit of everything. Just a taste. Just enough to know he'd been there.

When he was fourteen years old, he went to God and asked Him to hear his prayer. God consented. Ralph said, "Lord, I know I don't deserve much. And I don't expect a lot. But I would like some things. Just a little bit. This is my request: I'd like my own bedroom away from my brother, some nice furniture, a stocked refrigerator, a boom box, a girlfriend with looks, and a pet or two. I'd like just a little bit of everything that's worthwhile. Please understand, I'm not asking for everything. Just a little bit of everything."

God understood a person's wanting something in this world, needing a little piece of ground of your own. He'd been the one to promise Abraham, Isaac, and Jacob a place. He didn't begrudge a man the basic needs, so He answered Ralph's prayer. He led his parents to give him his own room, a little fridge all his own, a dog, and one of the cheerleaders fell in love with him. Also, he got two pairs of designer jeans, a toaster, a color TV, a stereo and record collection (not the top of the line, mind you, but square middle of the store), and a boom box for the beach. It wasn't the American dream, but it was comfortable. Ralph was pleased.

Nonetheless, after a few years of living in the lap of mediocrity, Ralph Pyle suddenly decided he wasn't fully satisfied. "What I need is the right to call some shots," he said. "Not all the shots—just some of them. I don't like people bossing me around all the time."

He journeyed again to the throne of God and set forth his plea. God listened and asked, "What kind of shots do you want to call? Basketball shots? Financial shots? Political shots? People to command and lead? A voice in your church?"

"That's it," said Ralph. "A little bit of all the above."

God answered quickly. Within a month, Ralph was signed up to vote on a special board at his church. He was also asked to represent the student body at the local PTA meetings. He was nominated for a position in his homeroom class. He became an assistant coach on the basketball team. And he got a job as a trainee at a local hamburger chain restaurant.

Ralph was happy. He knew he wasn't a particularly ambitious guy, not like some of the guys he met. They awoke early, came home late, and never seemed to get a moment's rest. But Ralph took naps. His parents listened to him. The dog sat when he said, "Sit." The people on the youth board listened to his advice. The local politicians thought he was fine. He was very happy.

But as always, the day came when Ralph sensed something else was missing. He began to realize a little bit of wealth and a chance to call some shots weren't all they were cracked up to be. He contemplated his problem, and he realized, "I don't have any notoriety, no fame. No one knows who I am, except, of course, my parents, and a few of the locals. I think if I had a little taste of fame, just a little piece of it, I would be completed."

Again, he set out for God's throne to lay his request at His feet. At first God didn't understand. "I know who you are," He said.

"But this is different," Ralph said. "I'd like to see my name in print. It would be nice if some people around town recognized me. I'd like them to say, 'There goes Ralph Pyle.'"

During the next few years, Ralph had the time of his life. One day when he was walking along the street with his dog, a channel 11 news truck stopped, and a reporter interviewed him about a community problem. He didn't know a lot about it, but he knew a little bit, and he told the reporter what he knew. He was on TV that night. The reporter even said, "You've given me some good quotes."

Later, his picture was in the paper when he received an award for his work as a trainer for the football team. His fiancée cut it out and put it in her scrapbook. People began to take note of Ralph Pyle. Not many people. But a few. Just enough to give Ralph a taste. Even Mrs. Hobson greeted him at the market, saying, "Why, I saw your picture in the paper, Mr. Ralph Pyle."

He said, "It wasn't such a good photo."

"Oh, I thought it was most handsome. It's not everyone who gets his picture in the paper."

And Mrs. Hobson had even fired him when he was younger for not cutting her lawn properly. It felt good to have her congratulate him.

Ralph was getting into his early twenties now, and he realized something remained wrong. "I have a little bit of wealth, power, and fame. But something's missing."

He thought for nearly a month. He observed some religious folks who didn't seem to have a care in the world. "Peace," he said. "I lack internal peace."

As he observed these people, he noted that they were the kind of fanatical religious folk he had never liked. Always helping the poor. Arguments about religion. Always telling people about sin. Ralph thought for a while before he went to God this time. But finally he did.

"Lord," he said, "I'd like some peace. Peace of mind. Peace of heart. But I don't want it to the point where I have to start telling people about sin. I don't want to be a fanatic. But I would like a little peace. Not a lot. Not much. Just a taste."

God sat for a long time before saying a word. Finally, He sighed. "Ralph Pyle, you have asked a hard thing. But there have been many who wanted such peace and, as always, I've done My best. What you want, I suppose, is to feel good about yourself, correct?"

Ralph nodded. "That's it! You put it so well."

God was dismayed, but He waved Ralph away, saying, "Go your way. I will send you such peace."

No prayer was ever answered so quickly. That week, Ralph went to a self-image seminar. Afterward, he felt so good he took his fiancée out to dinner.

A few weeks later, he listened to some tapes by a famous television preacher. After that, he was so positive and inspired that his family wondered what had happened to their somber son and brother. Finally, he bought some books about guilt. After learning the formulas and applying a few of them, he felt such relief that he nearly walked on air. He felt good about himself.

However, as always, Ralph noticed things weren't right. It just wasn't enough. Something was definitely absent. This time he thought for nearly three months. He even went to the pastor for some counseling.

Through his advice and Ralph's own personal insights, he came to the conclusion that what he lacked was love. He'd never really experienced love—not like in the movies. Oh, he thought highly of his fiancée. She was pretty and loving, and she knew how to kiss. But she nagged him now and then. And occasionally they had fights. He liked his family a lot. But they were often a bother, especially when he wanted to listen to music in his room. He wanted to feel real love for everyone.

He went to God again and laid it all out before Him.

"You mean you want to be able to love like the nuns in Calcutta who take care of lepers?" God asked, excitedly.

Ralph crinkled up his eyes. "I wasn't thinking of that."

"Then you must mean you want to learn to be patient, kind, not jealous, and so on?" God asked again.

Ralph cocked his head. "In a way," he said. "But I wouldn't want it to become a bother. I mean, I wouldn't want to have to go out of my way all the time."

God appeared to be dismayed, but He asked one last question. "I guess you don't mean the kind of love that leads a person to give up his whole bank account to help someone in need?"

"Oh, no," said Ralph. "Not that. It's . . . it's the kind of love . . . "

166

" . . . that has a warm feeling in your heart for everyone," said God, completing the sentence.

"That's it!" said Ralph, looking up. "How did you know?"

God sighed deeply. "You ask a hard thing, Ralph Pyle. I know the kind of love you want. I've seen much of it. I guess I've always found a way to supply it. So why not for you?" He said, shaking his head. "Go your way. I'll try to answer."

This answer was slow in coming. Gradually, Ralph noticed that he began to have nice feelings toward some people. He found that he actually liked a lot of people. Not to the point that he really did anything for them. But he began to describe himself as a humanitarian. "I care about the race," he said. "I hope we all get it together."

Sometimes he thought about writing a letter to his congressman about some problem. On one occasion, he even gave a little money to an organization that helped orphans. He felt great after that. He became a nice guy.

Of course, it wasn't enough. He was nearly thirty, and he still lacked something. After nearly a year of thinking about it, one morning it hit him. "I don't have faith," he exclaimed to his wife. "I lack faith. I must go to God and talk with Him immediately about it."

Before he went, he decided to read the Bible. For many hours he meditated on such statements as, "Unless you take up your cross and follow after Me, you are not worthy of Me." And, "Take My yoke upon you and learn of Me, for I am gentle and humble in heart." He also watched Christians—in church, out of church, in the home, out of the home.

Finally, he formed his petition. "I lack faith," he told the Almighty. "I want some faith."

"Do you want the faith that moves mountains?" asked God, pleased.

"Oh, not all that much," said Ralph, smiling. "I just want enough faith to get me to heaven."

God's face became dark. "Do you not want the faith that takes up its cross and follows My Son wherever He goes?"

"Not that much," replied Ralph. "Just enough to keep me out of hell."

167

God appeared angry, but Ralph kept smiling. God had done everything else he'd asked.

"Do you want the faith that obeys My Word, studies My truth, and yearns for righteousness, meekness, and abundant life?"

Ralph said, "The abundant life part, yes. But those other things I don't think I really need. I just want enough faith to make me a decent American."

God sighed a long, heavy, dark sigh. He said, "Ralph Pyle, you ask the impossible. There is no such faith."

Ralph laughed. "That cannot be, Your Majesty. I see this faith everywhere I go."

God shook his head. "Yes, you have seen it. But you have not seen faith. What you ask is impossible. I can give you no such faith. Go your way."

At first, Ralph was greatly dismayed. But then he said to himself, "God can't be right. All these people can't be wrong. Maybe He just had a bad day."

So Ralph found his own faith. It was a rather fun faith. He was always asking God to do things after that: relieve a headache, get him a raise at work, find a parking space on a crowded Saturday. Sometimes God answered; sometimes He didn't. But when He did, Ralph was always pleased and even told the church about it. He became one of the church's best members.

But it wasn't enough faith to get him to heaven. It wasn't enough to keep him out of hell. It was just enough to make him think he had it made. And that he had a little bit of everything.

21
Pits

How Holmes had gotten into the pit he couldn't explain. He'd been there ever since he could remember. His mother had been there. And his father, brothers, and sisters.

It wasn't such a bad place. Jagged crags jutted up above him. The sun shone down and illuminated everything. Sometimes it was unbearably hot, but a tree at the edge of the pit provided some shade, and it wasn't too unpleasant.

He'd tried to climb out many times. But it was quite impossible. The sides of the pit cut his hands and feet. Where he could get a fingerhold, he was as likely to lose a fingertip as to hold on. In other places, the walls were smooth and sheer as the slabs of shale on the floor of the pit. It was no use. Climbing out wasn't the way.

But Holmes wanted out. He hated the pit. It was desolate, lonely. For years he'd told himself that it was OK, that he could make it. "Just cope," he said to himself. "Don't fret about it. No one else has it any better." But something within him thought that life had to be better than this.

One day a man appeared on the edge of the pit. He looked down and spied Holmes instantly. "So you're in the pit," he said.

"What's it look like?" answered Holmes, cheerlessly. "You know a way out?"

The man nodded. "I'm a great believer in the truths of the Buddha. They'll help you get out of the pit."

Holmes became excited. "What do I do? Tell me."

The man said, "It's simple. You must overcome all desire. Follow the eightfold path, and you will break the endless cycle of karma. Your soul will be set free, and you'll be out of the pit, even though your body will still be in it."

Holmes slit his eyes. "My soul set free but my body still here? What kind of nonsense is that?"

"No nonsense. Just meditate. Eliminate all desire. Your suffering will end." The man left.

Holmes snorted. "I guess I can't lose anything trying this." He plopped himself down and tried to clear his mind. "I will think of nothing, do nothing, be nothing," he said. "I will end my suffering by eliminating all desire."

He concentrated. But it seemed his desire to escape the pit only magnified. The more he tried to eliminate desire, the more powerful it grew until his mind seethed with a single passion to get out, to get away, to leap out of the pit. After several hours of struggle and failure, he gave up. At that moment he spotted another man passing by the edge of the pit.

"Hey!" yelled Holmes. "Do you have any ideas about how to get out of the pit?"

The fellow was wearing a yellow robe and appeared to be bald. "Of course. All you have to do is chant this little chant I learned, and everything will be OK."

"What is it?" Holmes wiped his forehead. It was hot.

"Hare Krishna, Hare Krishna, Hare Rama, Hare Rama. Just say it about three thousand times a day."

"Why?"

"It'll make you happy."

Holmes slumped. "I don't want to be happy. I want to be out of the pit."

The fellow yawned. "Sorry. Our book doesn't say anything about pits. Just about how to be happy." He wandered off, and Holmes was alone again.

"Creep!" he shouted.

Suddenly, a bearded man with a notebook appeared above him and gazed at the hapless Holmes. "Can I offer you my services?"

"Who are you?"

"A scientist," he said. "And a doctor of engineering."

"Fantastic!" said Holmes. "Can you engineer a way out of the pit?"

The scientist looked around. "I think so. I've built such contraptions before. Let me see what I can do."

The scientist brought in a team of students who began putting together a marvelous piece of machinery. In no time the scientist had dropped it in by parachute with a full manual and list of instructions.

"How do I work it?" shouted Holmes.

"Read the directions," said the scientist and headed off down the road.

Holmes read. And read. And read. He tried this button and that lever. Nothing happened. Then he found the electrical cable.

"There's nowhere down here to plug it in!" he cried.

No one answered.

Holmes shouted again, but all he heard was his voice echoing. "Great!" he said. "Now I'm not only not out of the pit, but now everything is cluttered up."

He sat down and banged his fist on the ground. "I'll never get out of here."

"I can help," said a smooth voice. A man with a vast smile appeared on the edge of the pit. "If you think you can, you can!" said the man.

"What do you mean by that?" Holmes was intrigued.

The man spoke, but his smile didn't move at all. "You must think in terms of possibilities, for all things are possible to him who thinks he can."

"What's the possibility of my getting out of the pit?"

"Just decide in your mind that you can do it," said the smiling figure, "and you'll do it."

"So what do I do now?" asked Holmes.

The man smiled vastly. "Plan. If you fail to plan, you plan to fail. But if you plan to win, your plan will win!"

Holmes felt a bit frustrated. "Will you please speak English? I want to get out of the pit."

"Plan your work, and work your plan," said the man.

"I don't have a plan," shouted Holmes. "And nothing has worked."

"Tut, tut," the man said. "Let me show you a few examples of those who have succeeded against all odds by using these principles." The man brought out three people who testified to the power of the principles. One had been poor, the second had suffered from depression, the third used to have a poor self-image. All had succeeded by right thinking.

Holmes interrupted. "Look, my problem isn't thinking. It's the pit. I want to get out of it."

The man threw him a book called *Success Unlimited* and said, "You can get other books at the bookstore."

Holmes shouted, "I can't even get to the bookstore!" But the smiling fellow was gone.

He stomped about in the bottom of the pit, pounding his fist into his palm and muttering.

Then he saw another man. He peered down, and Holmes was about to speak, but the man simply clambered over the edge of the pit and begin climbing down. Holmes watched with fascination. The man found handholds and footholds where there had been sheer rock before. As he drew near, Holmes noticed that his back was bent and torn. His hands and feet had great scars on them.

"He must be used to climbing into pits," Holmes said to himself.

It was only minutes until the man stood before him. "Get on my back," he said.

Holmes was about to protest, but the man's face was so utterly sincere that the hesitation and fear left him. He jumped onto his back, then gripped him with his arms and knees.

The man began climbing. Holmes marveled as he watched him pick his way upward. He climbed smoothly, effortlessly from Holmes' point of view, but many times the man cried out in pain. When they reached the top, his fingers were bloody.

Holmes hopped off and said with care, "Can I bandage your wounds?" The man held out his hands, and Holmes made a dressing from some fresh grass and leaves. When he finished, the joy of being out of the pit struck him. He stood to

172

suck in the cool air. "I can't believe it—I'm out. It was that simple. How can I thank you?"

"Just say it," he said.

Holmes laughed. "That's all? Just say 'thank you'?"

The man smiled and nodded.

Holmes thanked him and paused. "But how can I ever repay you?"

The man smiled again. "You can't."

He jolted at this blunt honesty. But suddenly, he understood and said, "That's a strange answer, but you're right. I can't repay you. I can only thank you." Holmes gazed at the man, perplexed. It had been so simple, so matter-of-fact. "Why did you do this? Why did you come down to get me?"

"Because I love you."

Holmes shook his head. "I don't understand."

"You will." The man got up and began walking away.

Holmes ran after him. "Wait, where are you going?"

"There are other pits, other people."

"But what should I do?"

The man turned, his eyes piercing Holmes to the heart. "Follow me."

Holmes's heart jumped. He stood staring back at the pit and at the vast landscape before him. "I could just go my own way," he muttered. "Why should I follow him?"

But something within him said there was much more to this than just being free. "I've got to find out more about this man," Holmes said to himself. He joined the man. "What's your name?"

"I am who I am," he said. "But you may call me 'Lord.'"

Holmes nodded and began gazing around him at the countryside. "It's so beautiful," he said. "I never knew it was like this." He looked into the Lord's eyes, and his mind seemed to fill with enormous thoughts, too great to contain. His heart swelled within him.

"This can't be," he said. "I must be half crazy. I'm beginning to think you're much more than a person who climbs down into pits."

"I am."

"Who are you?"

"I am the bread of life, the resurrection, the way, and the truth. But you can't understand all this now. You have to grow."

"I suppose you're right. I want to learn from you. I will follow you. But what do I do?"

Suddenly, a cry pierced the air. "Help, I'm in the pit!"

Holmes thought a moment. Then he leaped up. "That's it, Lord! I'll look for people in pits, and you can come to rescue them."

The Lord laughed and motioned with his arm. "Do it."

Holmes ran in the direction of the voice. In only moments he found a man in a pit much like his own. He shouted down to the man that help was coming. Then he looked toward Lord and cried, "Over here, Lord. This guy is really desperate."

22
Skirt and Flirt

Ben O'Day sat staring into the dying embers of the late night fire. He had to admit, the meeting had been good, better than he'd expected. For once, he'd understood the preacher. He recalled times without number of going to church and being bored to numbness.

This evangelist had been different. He had called for a decision.

Ben reflected on his words. "Some of you will go out of here tonight and will not be alive tomorrow. I plead with you, believe on the Lord Jesus Christ, and you shall be saved. Call upon Him in prayer. Trust Him. He is the God of heaven, the Lord of the universe. He's your only hope."

Ben watched the log break in a shower of sparks. The fire settled down to a strident glow.

I've never really believed in Jesus, he thought. *I know I'm no Christian. It's got to be something you experience. But it all seems so . . .*

Useless?

"Yeah, useless," he said in agreement. He rubbed his lower lip with his hand, a characteristic gesture when he was thinking deeply.

What if I just knelt here by the couch and prayed? he mused. *I wonder if it would do any good.*

Sure, go ahead. Do it. It won't hurt anything.

Ben laughed. "That must be my conscience speaking. Well, I'm going to think on this one before I do anything. All right?"

He nestled down in the sofa and picked up a pillow to hold over his chest. He thought about the many times he'd heard "the gospel" and "the truth." Every time there was something inside him that pushed it away. All those teachers with their little bunnies and flannelgraph stories and the big pictures of Jesus feeding the five thousand, pictures filled with sheep and lambs and children. It had all seemed to stupid, so far away from the real world.

But what if there really is a God? What if Jesus was God? What then?

He waited for some thought to register in his mind. Nothing came to him. The issue of God always troubled Ben. How could anyone know He was there, alive, real? How could anyone be sure Jesus was who they said He was?

You could do something about it.

But what?

You could decide to believe it.

Really?

Absolutely . . .

Yes?

Of course, it would only be one of many such beliefs.

That's true.

There are other important things.

Yeah.

Like what?

Oh, lots of things. Music. I love music. That's important. I can get into a good tune any time. And my work. I love my work. I might even be able to make a mark, leave the company in better shape than I found it.

Anything else?

Sarah. She's important. I'll probably marry her. One of these days anyway.

You know, you're not a bad guy, Ben O'Day.

Ben chuckled. "Now I know this isn't my conscience! This must be the devil."

Yeah, right.

Ben relaxed a little. He put his feet up on the little leather stool and pressed his fingertips against one another. He liked the tension. It felt good to force back his fingers, stretch them, push against the power in his hand.

But he especially liked knocking an idea around in his head.

How about a little mental exercise?

Sure.

A man has seventeen camels and three sons. To the first, he wants to give one half of the inheritance . . .

Come on, I already know the solution to that one. Give me something hard.

All right. What's the correct religion? Which one is right?

That's easy. All of them. They're all ways to God.

Well, that was simple enough.

Give me something harder.

Who was Jesus?

Well, if you were to ask the preacher tonight, he'd say that He was the Son of God, the Savior of the world, the one way, truth, and life. All that.

Excellent! You're really grappling with the hard stuff.

Ben laughed again. He heard his mother come in.

"Hi, hon."

"Hi, Mom. How're you doing?"

"Oh, fine. Just tired."

"Tough day?"

"They're all tough."

You ought to go give her a hug. She needs it.

Ben got up and walked over to his mom. "Let me help you off with your coat."

She glanced at him incredulously and said, "What's gotten into you? Did you get some religion at the church tonight?"

Ben laughed. "No, just thought I'd let you know I love you."

And give her a hug.

After taking off his mother's coat, Ben gave her a zesty hug.

"To what do I owe all this affection?"

"Just write it off to growing up and appreciation."

You really know how to make a mom feel good.

Ben smiled.

"Would you like some tea?" his mother asked.

"Sure. And some popcorn."

She disappeared into the kitchen. Ben went back out and looked at the fire.

But what if Jesus really was the Son of God?

Good question. But . . .

Probably unanswerable. Right?

You might be surprised at the answer to that one, so I'll have to think about it.

OK, let's get down to the real issues then. If Christ was the Son of God, if He was really God incarnate, then that means I owe Him something—everything. Correct?

Correct.

But it's a moot point. Who knows the answer? I sure don't.

Ben's mother walked in with the tea. "So how was the service tonight?"

"Not bad."

"Did you learn anything interesting?"

"It was the usual stuff."

"Anyone go forward and repent?" Ben heard the sarcasm in his mother's voice. She had no faith of her own, and she didn't like to see it developing in her son.

Ben sipped his tea. It was hot but delicious, a honeyed, spiced warmth drifting into his nostrils. He lay back and breathed in deeply.

"Nothing like some good spiced tea to get you back to reality," his mother said.

"Yeah."

Ben thought back over the years. He remembered how, when he was a child, his dad had made all the family go to church. Then his father had died when he was fourteen. His mother didn't make anyone go after that, nor would she go herself. He knew she felt a lot of bitterness about it. At the funeral the pastor had spoken of the wisdom and love of God.

But it had made no sense to him at the time and certainly not to his mother.

She pulled out a novel she had been reading, a thriller. "Is it good?" Ben asked.

"Not as good as his others. But passable. Better than most of what you get nowadays on the rest of the rack." His mother liked thrillers, suspense, the long reads that built to a towering conclusion.

Ben sank back and sipped the tea again.

So where were we?

The meaning of the universe.

Oh, it wasn't that heavy.

Pick a subject.

Repentance.

I was just going to suggest it.

What is it?

You don't know?

How am I supposed to know?

It's rather crucial, wouldn't you say?

Crucial?

Absolutely. If you don't get that one, you get nowhere.

You're talking in circles again.

Not at all. Repentance is the back side of faith. With faith you believe and commit yourself to those beliefs. Repentance is the other side. You turn from false beliefs and sin, of course.

Sin?

Absolutely.

Like what?

Drinking. Sleeping around. Smoking pot.

I'd have to give all that up?

Of course.

That's tough.

Hey, friend, this is serious business. You'd better reckon with it.

Ben swallowed and watched his mother over the edge of his mug. He liked the inner bantering, but he was never sure how much of it was himself, and how much was . . .

What?

179

Tell me. Be honest. Where does this voice come from? Is it just inside myself? Or is it the voice of God? Or . . .

Or?

Or the voice of someone else?

What do you think?

I think it's the devil.

Then I'm caught. Caught dead square on Boardwalk with two hotels.

Ben laughed. *Ah, it's just my own thoughts. Good grief, here I am thinking there's devils and demons. Soon I'll be having a seance.*

Ben's mother looked up. "A private joke?"

Ben smiled. "Just thinking, Mom."

"Well, be careful. Don't blow a cylinder."

Ben got up. "Do we have a Bible around here?"

"Oh, no, the boy has been converted!"

"No, Mom. I'm just interested. Where's my old Bible?"

"You'll have to look for it. I honestly don't know. But if you start acting like some kind of holy roller, you're going to have to find another place to live."

Ben began walking upstairs.

There's some cake in the kitchen.

Oh, yeah, I was going to scarf up some of the Chocolate Thrill Mom makes.

Ben turned around and headed for the kitchen. He cut a slice, then called to his mother to see if she wanted a piece. She didn't. He sat at the table.

Now what was I thinking about?

Repentance.

Oh, yeah.

It's a complete turnaround.

Yeah, I don't think I'm ready for that yet.

Ben noticed the evening paper on the table and began perusing the headlines.

In what seemed only moments, an hour had passed and he was ready for bed.

Well, I guess I'll have to think about this some more tomorrow.

180

I'll be here.
Yeah, I know.

"Tough day, Gam?"
Yeah. Rough.
"What went on?"
The usual.
"What's that?"
Mind games. He likes mind games.
"What's the problem?"
I feel like I'm walking a tightrope through Enemy territory.
"You've got to find what they like, Gam. That's the game."
I know. I know. But it's nerve-racking. Really nerve-racking.
"Ah, don't worry about it. One day he'll be dead, and you won't have to skirt and flirt anymore. Right?"
Right.

Ends

23
The Count

David Leene bent over the books once again. "I can't believe it," he murmured. "Our profits are up three hundred percent in less than a year."

He had already checked the numbers twice. When his accountant first rushed in to inform him, he was skeptical. But now he was convinced. "There's no question what I'll do now," he said to himself. "It'll be four more franchises in P.A., and one each in N.J., M.D., and D.C." He reflected on his unique way of referring to the states of his homeland. One of the little trademarks he was known for in the business.

He had a multitude of such idiosyncrasies. The cigar trick was his best. After concluding a big deal, he'd take the corporate brass out to a restaurant, throw a rich repast, and finally pass out thick Cuban stogies wrapped in twenty dollar bills. Then he'd stand and say, "You can keep the twenty if you want, gentleman, but my preference is that you use it to light this delicate little instrument of pleasure. Once you install my equipment in your factories, you'll soon be lighting up hundred dollar bills."

The results became the byword of the business. "If Leene's machines don't get you in the black, then send them back, and no flak, Jack."

David Leene laid back in his chair and laughed. *I ought to retire,* he mused. *That would be the greatest heist of all. I can see the headlines. "Leene Retires After 300% Year." I keep my hand in it by holding the stock. But no more running. I have to take my ease sometime. Do some feasting. I've had my nose to the stone for so long it doesn't even itch anymore.*

As Leene thought, he became drowsy. His eyelids sagged. In moments, he was snoring in the leather, burgundy-dyed chair, as unassuming and relaxed as a sparrow on a guy line.

Suddenly, a sharp sound penetrated his sleep, and he jolted awake. After glancing around, he mumbled, "Just the wind. What's gotten into you, Leene?"

But a strange shadow appeared from behind the curtains, and Leene's heart jumped. "Who's there?" he shouted. "I haven't invited anyone in here."

To his alarm, a voice answered. "I'm sorry. I wanted to get you while you were still asleep."

Leene jumped up and pulled open a drawer, grasping a pistol he kept there for security. He pointed the barrel toward the shadow, which was moving toward him.

"Who are you?" Leene cried, now frightened and white.

"Death," said the voice, quavery and crackly.

Leene laughed. "Death! This has got to be a dream. Wake up, you fool."

The shadow moved closer. "I'm sorry you are awake, though I had planned to get you while still asleep. I really hate these arguments, you know."

Leene swallowed. "You mean this is real? I've never heard about anything like this."

The shadow moved as though a head were shaking. "That's why I prefer to get them while they're asleep. Most people complain profusely about it, making threats, screaming, claiming it's unfair, and so forth. Anyway, I wish I could wait, but I have to begin the count now, or I'll be late. So if you don't mind, ten, nine . . . "

Leene backed up as the shadow moved forward. "What are you doing? What do you mean 'count'? Am I about to die?"

"Yes. Eight, seven . . . "

"Hold it!" shouted Leene. His voice echoed, and he jumped at its sound. But instantly he returned to the shadow, trying to make out a shape or face. "Look, I don't know what you're doing, but I think I ought to at least have an explanation. What's this all about?"

Death sighed. "This is the way these things are carried out. I simply count you out. It's similar to the thing your referees do with boxers, only, of course, this is a much more solemn affair. I hate to turn it into a circus. But, you see, I have to be precise about these things. You know what it says, I assume: 'It is appointed unto man once to die.' The appointments are fixed and precise to the second, so I'm always careful to do a count. It helps me keep things on schedule."

Leene's shoulders slumped as Death spoke. Death's voice chilled him through. It was like freezing cold on his face. At the same time, it made him sleepy.

Death said, "Anyway, if you don't mind, I'll continue. Six..."

The number rang out like a shot. Leene leaped back to full alert. "This isn't right," he seethed. "You have no right. I'm not ready to die. My company just tripled its profits. I've got things to do. You'll have to change your schedule."

Death shook his head with frustration. "What makes you think these things can be changed? It's not as though you're in charge here."

Now Leene was angry. "This is my office," he said, "and I haven't asked you here. I think you'd better go."

"Five..."

Leene leaped forward at the shadow, trying to grab it. But it seemed to surround him.

"Who do you think you are?" he shouted. "I'm not a person to be toyed with. If you really want to take me, then at least serve notice, and give me several days to think about it."

"It's not done that way," Death said, patiently. "I come when I'm told, no sooner or later. And you don't do the telling."

"Then who does? Tell me that. I'd like to speak to him."

Death sighed again. "You'll be appearing before Him soon enough," he said. "Four..."

"And who is He—God, I suppose?" Leene said sarcastically. "Well, I don't believe in Him."

"That doesn't matter," said Death. "Personal preferences and ideas about God don't change who or what He is."

For a moment, Leene was stunned. Somehow he'd always thought that one's belief or lack of it was the determining factor. But he was angry. He replied, "Well, then, He should have informed me about Himself. If He's so sure about His existence, why didn't He make me sure?"

Death's voice continued to intone with patience. "Don't you have a Bible? Yes, I see it over on the shelf there. Aren't there churches in this neighborhood? Yes, I passed three on this very street. Hasn't your wife repeatedly expressed to you a desire that you repent and believe in Jesus? Of course. My records show, in fact, that various other relatives, several local pastors, two young people in your company, a man in your lodge, several people on the street, and numerous others have all mentioned to you the need to believe and follow Christ. In each case, your conscience also reminded you to listen."

Leene sputtered and shook his head, but Death continued. "In addition, our records show that more than eight hundred thousand times—803,674 to be exact—throughout your sixty-five years on earth, you were reminded about wrong actions of every sort. In each case, it was recorded that according to principle your conscience told you that what you were doing was wrong both before, during, and after the acts of sin. It is also written that you only changed your actions under threat of punishment, and that was only in a few cases."

Leene clenched and unclenched his fist around the handle of his pistol. "I suppose you know all about me. Then tell me this, Know-it-all, what about when I went forward for baptism in my church when I was twelve? Doesn't that count for anything?"

Death wheezed a lengthy sigh. "The records show that this particular act was motivated by a desire to gain a certain medal in your Boy Scout troop."

"A lie!" shouted Leene. "You have no proof of that."

"Look," said Death. "I have a long night ahead of me. My responsibility is not to prove anything. That will all be taken care of. I really do have to get on with this. If you had considered that I would come someday, you might have been better prepared."

Leene's mouth dropped. "Better prepared? How did I know you were coming? You never sent me a note. You never called me on the phone."

Death replied, "Every time you went to a funeral, every time you passed a graveyard, every time you had a brush with disaster, I reminded you. In fact, as the years have passed, my reminders have begun to come daily. But you usually listened for a moment and said, 'It's a long way off.' Well, I'm sorry, but today is the day. I've done my best. I run an honest service here. Now, I've got to get back to the count. Three ..."

"But what about the millions who haven't heard? I suppose they get the same treatment, but they don't even have a chance."

"First," said Death, "my Master always deals with everyone with perfect justice. So you can leave the matter of those who haven't heard to Him. Second, you have heard. You're responsible for yourself, not them. This is taking a bit longer than I'd planned. I really have to move on."

Leene pointed the gun at the shadow. But he realized such a tactic was useless. Suddenly, an idea hit him. "Look, Death, I've heard of people being saved at the last minute, on their deathbeds. Is that possible?"

Death was quiet a moment. He said, "Yes, it's possible. I'm not usually one to say such things, but all things are possible with Him. I'm seen many 'deathbed conversions' as they're called. There's always time to repent and believe as long as you're alive."

"Then I could do it right now, right?"

"Of course. Any time, so long as you're still alive. I would be glad to see it." Death waited.

Leene screwed up his face through several contortions, but somehow the more he thought about repenting, the angrier he became. He found himself thinking, *What right does God have to demand this of me? Why should I repent now? This is preposterous. I've always hated this kind of thing, and I'm not going to indulge in such nonsense now.*

189

He turned again to Death. "Death, I need more time to think. I haven't had enough time. Come back tomorrow."

"I'm sorry," said Death. "As I understand it, He gives each person precisely the time they need. If they don't do it by then, they'll never do it. So please allow me to do my duty. One . . ."

Leene fell to his knees. "Please, Death, I will repent. Just give me one more hour."

The shadow moved quickly and enveloped Leene. Leene fired the gun. Death quietly said, "Zero," and as Leene slumped to the floor, Death glanced at Leene's watch and nodded.

Once again he had performed his service on the dot.

The next day the story took up a minute in the nightly news. It was mentioned that Leene had had a 300 percent year and that there had been a strange gunshot the night he died. But the investigators had come up with no clues as to whether an intruder had come into Leene's office. The anchorman even lit a cigar with a twenty-dollar bill in Leene's honor. Turning to the weatherman, he remarked, "I guess when your number's up, it's up, isn't it, Bill?"

"Yep," said the weatherman, turning to the camera. "And your number may be up this weekend, folks, 'cause we've got a doosie for you."

24
Before the Great Seat

The group was rather grim, even though the robes were nice. Someone said, "They're special—keep your defects from showing."

"Defects?" I asked.

"Sin," he said and laughed. "He can't bear the sight of it."

I grimaced.

Another whispered to me. "Who cares about the robes? They're saying today's the day."

What day? But this time I didn't ask. I already knew. I'd known about it for—ever since I'd left—where was it? Earth. Yes, earth. Ever since. But I had never really believed it. It couldn't be as bad as some were saying.

"All of us condemned," some were saying. "Nobody will be let in."

"Ha!" a fellow near me cried. "I'd like to see that. All of us? Forget it. Not me. Not this little blue duck. You can forget that. I'll get in."

I wasn't afraid. Not at all. In fact, I had been waiting for this day. For—how long had it been?—maybe centuries now. This was the day we'd get it all straightened out. Settled. No more crying in the dark. No more threats. No more vengeful thoughts. "Let's get it all out, over and done with," I'd said to myself that very morning.

I was sure there wouldn't be much to it. It would be quite plain, once everything was laid out heaven-clear and bright in the sunlight. There would be no mistaking it. They'd see. He'd see. I'd be free of these chains.

Suddenly, there was a great quiet. "He's coming," someone whispered. When He arrived, He sat down on a monstrous throne. "A bit ostentatious," someone else whispered.

Another answered, "Shut up, you fool. Don't you know what this is about?"

"Yeah. What a laugh!"

The man next to me started to whimper. "I know something's going to go wrong. It won't work out like I planned."

I shrugged. "It'll work out. Watch. It'll be simple. We'll all get through. That is, except for a few. You know the ones I mean."

"Right," he said. "I've been waiting for one fellow to get his for a long time. It'll be nice to see him decked."

I smiled. I had my own list, too.

The Great One pulled out some books. Gigantic books. A whole library full. No, make that libraries. Cities of libraries. It was incredible. A whole world couldn't have held them.

Yet, somehow it didn't seem that important. Nor so big. What are books, anyway? Like I always said back on earth, "You can find a loophole for everything."

Even He didn't seem so big, once you got used to Him, sitting up there gazing at you. Every now and then His eyes met mine. I'd flinch away quickly. There was this burning sensation deep inside me. I didn't like it. I hoped whatever happened wouldn't mean I'd have to be around Him a lot. Or at all, for that matter. It would be nice if I didn't have to mess with Him at all.

His voice boomed out across the plain. "What kind of justice do you want—biased, or unbiased?"

He had to be kidding.

"Who does He think He is?" someone muttered to my left. "Doesn't He know we saw enough of the biased type on earth?"

"Unbiased, of course," yelled a large fellow. Someone told me he was Peter the Great, a Russian czar.

Someone else said, "Be careful, it might be a trick. You never know what He might do." (They said he was Napoleon, but . . . that small? Come on.)

Nevertheless, it was quickly settled. Unbiased justice was what we wanted. I was pleased. At last we were getting somewhere. He wasn't bad. Even a bit on the democratic side.

The Great One asked again, "Shall it be partial or complete?"

You had to think about that one. Admittedly, there were things I'd like to leave out. My own things. But when I thought about it—about some of the people I wanted to see get it good—I didn't want anything overlooked, even if it meant that for me. He might overlook that one point, that one speck that counted for me anyway. Just the same, it would have to be the same for all of us, I guessed. That was the way He was.

I wasn't afraid. Even though I'd done my share of deeds, evil and otherwise, I was sure there wasn't much He could pin on me. It was all perfectly logical. There were, of course, a few things, unmentionables, which no one but He knew about. And who knows, maybe even He didn't know. But if it came down to it, I could make a defense easily enough.

So we all agreed. "Complete," we said. Someone added, "We want every account settled. Nothing left open."

The Great One spoke again, "Shall it include every sinner or just selected ones?"

"So long as I'm not selected," shouted one man. We all laughed. Someone said he was Hemingway, but he didn't have a beard.

I had to admit, I had to think about this particular point. Finally, I asked, "Who would do the selecting?"

The Great One answered, "What do you think? Would you like to do it?"

People turned angrily in my direction, and embarrassed, I looked down. Someone answered, "Include every one, and make sure everyone's included."

The Great One answered, "I will."

After a few moments' pause, He asked, "Should I include every sin—deed, word, and thought—or just selected sins?"

This was nerve-racking. Why didn't He just get on with it? Every sin, of course. You can't leave anything out when you're planning to be just about it. Of course, you have to remember the good stuff, too. I didn't want any of that overlooked either.

I turned to the man next to me. He was excitable and didn't want to say anything. But I whispered, "You don't think He should leave anything out, do you?"

"Nah," he said, as he rubbed his jaw. "Leave it all in. Get it all finished with. That's what I say. I'm not ashamed of anything." But when he said it, he looked away, like he knew something else deep down.

No one had answered the Great One yet. We were all murmuring and talking together—checking to be sure we weren't making a mistake.

"Of course," said the excitable one, as he shifted nervously on his feet, "I hear that what we thought of as 'good' down there doesn't turn out to be so good up here."

"Oh, yeah?" I said suspiciously. I'd heard that too, but I couldn't see how. "What do you mean?"

"Don't know," said the man. His eye was twitching now. "It's just that He doesn't measure things the same way."

I shook my head. "A yardstick's a yardstick. How different can it be? I was pretty good compared to. . . . Well, you know what I mean."

"That's just it," he said. "I hear He doesn't compare us to each other."

I cringed. What did he mean by that? What other way was there to do it?

I realized deep down inside that what he said was true. I'd always known it was true, even though I'd tried to tell myself otherwise.

The nervous man said very low, "I just want to get it over with. It was getting cramped down there."

I agreed. The sooner the better.

When we had agreed that He should accept every sin and every good thing, He asked another question. "Shall the magnitude of the punishment be equal to the magnitude of the crime?"

194

On that there was little discussion. "Absolutely," we all said. A woman shouted out, "I was raped, and the rapist was a Babylonian soldier who was told to rape me. I want to see that made right. For all of them—from the king down through the officers, to that last one who actually did it!"

Another man cried, "My family was killed by the Huns. They came in and took everything, the murderers. I want justice. Complete. I want to see them burn!"

Soon, everyone was shouting out their own grievances. "I was murdered in an alley." "My father was taken by a cheat."

I joined in and reminded Him of several things. Somehow, in spite of our great numbers, it seemed that He took it all in, remembered everything. It was something about the way He looked at you when you spoke to Him. I couldn't pin it down. Almost as if He were determined to do what was right and best, no matter how long it took.

I thought there couldn't possibly be any more questioning, but the Great One went on, "Shall testimony include only the facts as witnessed by the eyes of Omniscience, or shall we consider fallible witnesses, as in an earthly court?"

Again, the answer was easy. I had been a lawyer. I knew what went on. Most of us had seen or been the victims of earth's justice. How they lied. How they cheated. How they bribed.

"The eyes of Omniscience!" one yelled.

Another agreed, "Omniscience!"

Soon everyone was shouting and jumping in their places. "Omniscience! Omniscience! Omniscience!"

It was a strange sensation. In one way I felt something inside my mind twisted into a contorted form of what I would have called "happiness" on earth. Yet something else within me was terribly afraid even as I shouted. I didn't know what it was, but there was rank terror inside me now.

When we calmed down, He gazed out at us for a long time. Finally, He said, "This last question is the most important one, and I want you to think about it before you answer. Shall the judgment be final with no appeals to lesser authority?"

We were all quiet. Suddenly, I realized how serious this all was. "Lesser authority"? What did He mean?

I gazed up at His face. So He really was the final and eternal authority. It hadn't struck me until now. He was the Supreme Court, the last stop, the final judgment.

Now, I understood that this One above all others was He who rules the universe with an iron hand. There was no one greater. "I never thought of it that way," I said to the nervous man next to me.

He quivered, then scoffed. "Don't fret. It'll all turn out. What're you shaking so badly for?"

I stared at him. Me, shaking? I looked around. All of us were trembling, even as we enthusiastically answered His questions. It was as if the answers were inevitable although we all knew exactly what they meant for each of us.

I shrugged. At least we'd arrived at a place where the die was cast and there was no turning back. At last, the crimes would be made right. At last, my heart would be at peace, knowing all the wrongs had been righted.

How was He going to do it? How could He make a just judgment with so many people and so many crimes? It seemed impossible and boggled my mind. I longed to see how justice would be meted out. This would be interesting, that was sure.

I was nearly jumping in place with excitement. It would really happen. It would soon be over. The criminals would truly get what they deserved. I wanted them all to face Him—all those mocking dictators, drug peddlers, cheats, murderers—all of them. I wanted to see them try to wriggle free this time—and be unable to.

I shouted, "Your judgment is final, Lord. There is no one else we'll appeal to."

The crowd joined in. "Your judgment, Lord. Yours alone."

The Great One stood. "Then we have agreed. The rules are settled. The judgment shall be unbiased, complete, and shall include all gathered here today. Every sin and every deed shall be considered and weighed. The magnitude of the punishment shall fit the crimes. Only the knowledge of the

Omniscient One will be used as testimony. And His judgment shall be final."

He paused and turned to His right. "Now I shall introduce you to the Judge. All kneel and bow."

As we knelt and bowed, my heart was pounding. He said, "Stand now."

The Judge stood before us. He was a man, or so He appeared. In one way He was terrible to behold, a man stern and silent who considered nothing but right. At the same time, you could see infinite compassion in His face. I trusted His judgment. I wanted Him to be my judge. I knew the Great One was right in choosing Him.

The Great One spoke again. "This is my beloved Son, with whom I am well pleased. You shall listen to Him and obey His judgment. When you approach the bench, you shall kneel before Him and bow. And you shall call Him 'Lord,' for so He is."

We all nodded.

He then said, "His name is Jesus."

Some gasped. Others continued to bow. I had known it all along, so it didn't trouble me much. I had no quarrel with Him, even if I had never really believed in Him or followed Him on earth. But many hadn't, so I expected that to be no problem.

The first one was brought forward. "Adam."

Adam! I was astonished. He was beginning at the beginning. Well, that was logical. It would be chronological, probably by date of birth.

No one came forward. The Judge said, "Check the Book of Life."

The recording angel looked into a huge book that was alone on a table to the right of the Judge. It was golden and full of light. I hadn't noticed it before.

The angel said, "Recorded, Lord. Redeemed. Everything already paid. Rewarded at the Bema."

Redeemed! Yes, I knew what that was. There was no need for an explanation. The whole thing on Calvary.

But an outcry arose from someone (they said it was Cain, Adam's son), "Where is he? Isn't he supposed to be here?"

197

"Everything has already been paid," said the Judge, holding up His hands. I noticed blazing red scars on them.

"How?" cried Cain.

"I paid it," said the Judge.

Cain slumped back. "What about me, then?"

"We will get to you," said the Judge. "Eve!"

The same process was repeated. And then we came to Cain. Cain stepped forward. "Jesus is Lord," he said with a bow.

The angel checked the Book of Life. "No name recorded," he said.

The Judge began unraveling all the mysteries of Cain's life—every deed, every word, every thought. It was both marvelous and pitiable. A horrid life, even before the murder of Abel. A despicable life. The Judge dealt with each deed, each thought, revealed it in the Light. The Light displayed Cain's callous refusal to believe, obey, or even listen to the Great One in any instance of his life. Even the good things—the well-farmed products, the honest bargaining—went awry. They had all been motivated by selfishness. Nothing hallowed. Nothing good or lasting. Nothing kind or giving or open or honest. All a cruel, unrelenting pursuit of self, his own kingdom, his own ways.

There was no mistaking it. Each part of his responsibility in the matters was weighed. The Judge considered his failures and successes. It was all clear. The utter failure, the ungodliness—all bloomed crystalline in the unflinching Light. At least in Cain's case, there could be no question.

The Judge pronounced His judgment. "Depart from Me," He said, "you who practice wickedness. "

All agreed. A horrid man. He got what he deserved.

Cain bowed again and said, "Jesus is Lord," then added, "You have done all things well. I accept Your judgment as complete and just."

It was astonishing. But as he was marched out of the chamber, hanging his head, it was obvious that no one could contradict the sentence.

I watched as hundreds, then thousands, were brought before Him, one at a time in order of their conception in time.

The book was checked. When someone was missing, he or she was discovered as already redeemed, sins paid for, rewarded at the Bema. But every time the name was not found, no questions were asked. No one disputed. No defense was attempted.

I watched with fascination and revulsion the revelation of things that had been done. So many secrets and foul deeds. Horrified gasps cut the quiet as the Judge revealed unknown realities.

Just the same, I always agreed with the Judge's judgment. He did not make a single error. The rules were kept. He was just, perfectly just.

And then I stood before Him. It seemed to go so quickly. I looked into His face. I was limp. All my plans suddenly vanished. To stare into His eyes was to see the absolute. I could praise Him for His perfection. He would be fair. No question about that. I would get whatever I deserved. Surely, it wouldn't be too bad.

The Book was opened. My name was not found in it. He then reviewed everything. I felt sick. In the Light it all looked so despicable, shriveled, ugly. It was all plain. Not one thought or deed possessed true righteousness. So much hatred, revenge, lust, anger, jealousy. Nothing clean anywhere.

The crowd was silent behind me. Of course, it had dwindled to a much smaller size by that point.

He looked into my eyes. "You never put your faith in Me when you lived on earth. Why?"

"It was too much trouble," I said, astonished at my own honesty. Could I be anything less than truthful to Him? "I didn't want to obey You. I didn't want Your rules. I wanted to live my own life."

"Do you remember My coming to you and telling you to turn, that time was running out?"

"Many times, especially in the last days."

"Why did you push Me away?"

I found myself struggling to drum up excuses. To say, "I never had the time" or, "It wasn't impressed on me strongly enough," or, "I didn't know enough." But all were untrue. I was incapable now of speaking anything but the truth. "Lord,"

I said, "I hated You. I hated everything You did and stood for. I wanted nothing to do with You. I wanted to do it my way, not Yours. Even now I want nothing to do with You. That is my desire."

It was a speech I'd heard every person before me make. I hadn't even noticed that every one of us had said virtually the same thing in our own words. Now I knew this was the crux of the issue.

He asked again, "But why did you reject My grace? Life, heaven, forgiveness were all My gifts. All you had to do was accept it. Why didn't you take it when I offered?"

Again, excuses flitted through my mind. It was too simple. It seemed preposterous. There had to be more. I said, "Because I didn't want to give up my sin. I preferred it to You."

He fixed His eyes on mine, and the fire seemed to burn through my soul. He said, "So you understand why I must make this final judgment?"

"Yes," I said and bowed. "You are Lord."

His face clouded, and as He looked into my eyes, I saw all that might have been. I saw beauty, joy, contentment. I saw Him as He was—loving, holy, magnificent, perfect. I saw that I had rejected it all and instead had won this, deserved this, must live with this judgment. Forever.

Yet, even now I wanted to get out of His revealing presence. Even now I hated Him, wanted nothing to do with Him.

He said, "Depart from Me, you who practice wickedness."

I looked at Him again and bowed. "Jesus is Lord. You have done all things well."

They led me out. I still hated Him. I wanted nothing to do with Him. But He had been just. Completely, perfectly, finally...

Just.

25
Defenses

Once there were four criminals sitting in their cells awaiting trial. Each tried to plan his defense, but ideas were short in coming. It looked like a closed and shut case to each of them.

As the first man pondered his situation, the devil appeared in his cell and said, "I think I can help. I have a defense for just the situation you are in. Would you care to try it?"

The despondent man leaped at the opportunity. The devil outlined an elaborate scheme. "I've heard about this judge," he said. "There's no getting at him with silver and gold. He already owns more than he can use. But I have a better plan. My philosophy is that everyone has his price, and he can be no different. Promise that you'll do good from now on. Say that you'll give to the poor. You'll work for an honest wage. You'll be kind to your wife. That will certainly melt his heart, for I have heard that he is compassionate in all instances."

The criminal's eyes lit with hope. He told the devil he'd use his words exactly. "Who knows," he said, "perhaps we'll find a sure way around this monster."

The day came for his trial, and the criminal appeared, eager to make his defense. The prosecution presented the evidence. No one refuted it. A gallery of onlookers sat in hushed awe at the prosecutor's dexterity. But the criminal rose in his place with confidence. "Your honor," he said, "we have all made mistakes. Perhaps even you, in your youth, have erred. But there is always room for a second chance."

The judge frowned, but he let the man go on. He proposed that he would first of all give to the poor. There being many poor people in the gallery, he sensed unspoken approval, though one old man wheezed, "I've heard that one before."

The criminal said he would work for an honest wage. Again, the gallery heads nodded, but one of the employers present laughed, "I've heard that one until I'm ready to start a one-man business!"

Finally, with a flourish of his hand to his wife in the wings, he said, "And above all, I promise that I will be kind to my wife."

The woman remained unimpressed and said, "He says that every time he comes home drunk."

But many agreed that this had been a good defense, and some bet in his favor.

However, the judge of all the earth rose from his throne and remarked, "I have heard these arguments before. I don't like them. They smack of arrogance."

The criminal began to stutter angrily, and at that point a baby crawled out of the gallery and began teething on his shoelace. When the criminal noticed him, he kicked at him and said, "I'm on trial for my life, and now I'm assaulted by slobbering children!"

The baby rolled over and began to wail, and his mother ran up and claimed him.

The judge pronounced the sentence, "I believe the facts —both past and present—speak for themselves. You are sentenced to the Labyrinth of Doom until every last cent is paid."

The criminal was dragged out, kicking and screaming.

Having heard of his fellow criminal's fate, the second criminal became even more despondent. Again, the devil appeared, saying, "I'm sorry about your friend. We can't always count on our tight arguments, for this judge is shrewd. But I have a second defense that is even better. Would you like to hear it?"

The criminal eagerly listened to the devil's thoughts, then began laughing in triumph. "Surely no judge even of all the earth will be able to withstand these sly words." And he proceeded to his trial with glee.

When it came time for his defense, the second man didn't wait. He said, "Judge, it is estimated that nearly seventy-five percent of our territories are populated by criminals, people awaiting trial for crimes such as mine. It would seem to me that there are many good lives—productive and worthwhile lives—represented here. It is inconceivable that so many good personalities should rot in the Labyrinth of Doom, for it is improbable that a man of your character would sentence so many to such a tragic end."

In his lengthy defense, the man turned several times to the devil in the gallery, who smiled and nodded him on.

"Therefore, I submit to you that you should simply let all go free on the basis of the fact that our numbers are so vast. It is unthinkable that you yourself should be bereft of so large and fine a contingent and that so many should waste away in oblivion when they can still live productively, despite their wrongs."

The gallery was dumb with wonder at the excellence of the argument and waited for the judge's reply. The judge stood and spoke, his eyes fiery: "You have erred, sir, in several ways. First, you think that mere numbers should prevent me from doing what is right. But what is right is right, regardless of how many follow it or don't."

Many in the gallery fell back with astonishment.

"Second, you seem to think that were there no citizens in the land after judgment I would somehow despair of having a friend. But I have friendship that you don't know about."

The criminal slumped in his seat.

"Finally, you claim that a man of my character would never do such a thing as judge millions because of the sheer waste. But, in fact, it is my character that requires such judgment, for such judgment is right, and I always do what is right."

The gavel crashed to the desk, and the criminal was taken away to the Labyrinth of Doom.

When the third criminal heard the news, he was near tears and suicide, but again the devil, trustworthy as ever, appeared and offered him a defense. "I have kept my best words for you. What do you say? Will you hear them?"

The man waved his hand listlessly, still feeling hopeless. But the devil told him the plot. "Tell the judge that you should indeed be banished from his territories for your crimes, but ask him to give you some new place to go, where you'll make a new start. Somewhere that you can be alone and think clearly. Another world, perhaps."

The criminal sat up and for the first time felt hopeful. He walked into the courtroom with a lightness of step. After he'd made his request, the judge asked him some questions.

"Where do you propose that I have this new world?"

The criminal felt greater confidence and said a bit flippantly, "I suppose it should be far away from you so that we wouldn't run into one another!"

The gallery laughed.

"And should this world contain anything of Mine so that I might rule it?" asked the judge.

"By no means," said the man, brightening. "We'll make of it what we can. Just leave everything to us."

The judge banged his gavel. "Indeed, you shall go to just such a world: the Labyrinth of Doom." The man began screaming even before they pulled him out of the courtroom.

When the devil came to the fourth man, he waved him away.

"You're not interested in my arguments?" he asked.

"I will plead the blood of Christ, Satan. Your words do not interest me."

"And how," said Satan, "do you think that will set you free?"

"The Judge has promised it," the criminal said.

The devil shrugged. "Play it your way, fool." He departed with smoke and stench.

When the criminal was dragged before the Judge, his defense was brief. "I know that you are righteous, O Judge, and that you never lie. I have lived a life of crime, as you well know. But You sent Your Son for me. I plead His blood and death as payment for my crimes. I have no other plea."

The Judge was obviously pleased, and the devil marked it from the gallery, where he watched the proceedings. The gavel resounded. "Case dismissed," said the Judge. "Enter into the joy of your salvation."

The gallery cheered. The criminal was given a new cloak and took his place with the company of heaven.

Then all were stunned to see the next defendant, who was the devil himself. He had been chained and muzzled, for it was said that he not only barked but bit. The Judge motioned with his hand, and the devil was freed.

"So you've brought me in at last," sneered Satan.

The Judge was silent for nearly a minute, then said, "State your case."

"Yes, I suppose that is what I must do like all the rest, isn't it?" he said, mockingly. "Well, here it is."

The whole gallery bent forward as one man. It was said that the devil was shrewd, sly, and rarely out-debated. Everyone knew well his own encounters with this fox. How would he wriggle out of the Judge's grasp? They'd never seen any escape, except those who pled the blood of Christ. But the devil surely couldn't plead that.

"Then," said the devil, "I plead the blood of Christ!"

The whole room reeled. Mouths popped open. A hush hung over the courtroom. All eyes turned quickly to the Judge. Would He have to let the devil go?

His face was impassive. "As a covering for your crimes?" He asked.

"Whatever," said the devil, with a flick of his wrist. "The same as the others."

"When was the blood applied to you?" asked the Judge.

The devil whispered to the gallery, "Since I realized nothing else worked," but no one laughed. He turned to the Judge, "I noted you didn't ask anyone else such questions when they pled the blood of Christ. I should think that being impartial, you would grant me the same right. My argument is the blood of Christ. If you accepted others, you must accept me."

The Judge leaned back on His bench. To the gallery, He appeared to be stymied. His face looked pale. None could see any way around it.

But He cocked His head slightly. His eyes were severe. "And just what has the blood of Christ done for you?"

The devil stamped his foot. "Why all the questions? I plead the blood of Christ. Am I set free or not?"

"Is there any reason you should not be set free, having pled the blood of Christ?" asked the Judge, His eyes glints of fire.

"How should I know?" shouted the devil. "You're the Judge. Make Your decision. This is my best argument."

The Judge leaned forward. "Did it occur to you, Satan, that the blood of Christ is not an argument or a strategy but eternal life itself? These are not the courts of earth!"

Instantly, the devil seemed to know it was over. "Then I'll hate You forever, You miserable . . . "

At that moment, one of the guards clapped the muzzle back on the devil's mouth. His words were muffled on the stiff leather.

"Take him away," said the Judge with a loud bang of the gavel. He then turned to the gallery. "Now, children, we shall celebrate."

26
Destiny

Consciousness slowly broke through the haze in Jeremiah Delms's mind. He had been sitting in church. Every Sunday he had occupied his usual seat: right side, fifth pew from the front, third person in. He had come to hear his wife's preacher. "Putting in my time," he always said. Even now he smiled.

But suddenly there had been pain in his chest, shortness of breath, no breath.

He had seen that great light—blinding, razing, hurling its rays like boulders. And he'd heard the voice. It had sounded awful, like a train slamming into a truck, and it had recapped his life, the whole sordid mess.

He wondered, *How did He know everything? Everything!*

Jeremiah had knelt before the voice, saying, "Your will be done." As if he'd had a choice. Then it was over. He had agreed. Justice was demanded and exacted.

But now his mind was filled with feathers on the wind. Each logical conclusion slipped away. He found himself dropped—no, falling—somewhere. Where?

"When it brightens up a bit, I'll take a look around," he murmured. His voice had a whispery sound, as when you think something so clearly it sounds as if you've said it out loud, but you know you didn't.

Jeremiah strained his eyes, looking to his left and right. Nothing.

"Where am I?" he repeated, this time quite distinctly. Again, his voice vanished with an eerie, shadowy tone, and he didn't know whether he'd thought or spoken the words. He shivered. "What is this nonsense?"

Ignoring the sound of his voice, he decided to begin to feel his way around. *I may be blind,* he thought. *Have to feel things. Maybe I've had an accident.*

He shoved his hand out into the darkness slowly. *You never know what you might strike if you do it too fast,* he thought. *Could hurt myself.*

Only moments before, he had begged—screamed—to get out of that scorching light. Now . . .

"God? Ha!" he cried. "I'm rid of You."

Moving around in the darkness, suddenly he trembled. His hand still seemed to be attached to him. He sensed its weight. But he found nothing to touch. He reached for his nose. It felt numb, but he knew it was there. It began to itch.

"My nose itches!" he shouted. The same shadowy shout. He tore at his face with his hands. No relief. He scratched violently, yet the itching sensation lingered.

He stopped, cocked his head, and listened. No sound—near, far, anywhere. No hum of traffic. No cricket chirps. No snoring, breathing.

"What about my voice?" he said. "There must be sound to it," he said. He whispered, "I'm here, all safe and sound." He let the *s*'s linger. But the sound seemed to disappear into the darkness, as though muffled in folds of cloth.

He shouted, "I'm here! I'm here! Where is everybody?" No one answered. Not even an echo.

He felt himself sweating. Instinctively, he raised his hand to his brow. But that same awful sensation of impotence gnawed at him. Beads of sweat slowly fell down his forehead, cheeks, and nose. Soon, his whole face prickled with hotness, wetness.

"A towel! I need a towel!" No answer. He bent down to feel madly along the bottom of wherever he was. There was no floor.

No floor! I'm standing on nothing. "But how?" he screamed. "How?"

208

Anger flashed through his body. His belly tightened, and a familiar pain struck his side—the perforated ulcer began to burn.

"I'll lie down," he said. "That always helped."

First he bent. Then he leaned. He was still upright. He curled into a ball and lunged—there was no up or down or sideways.

"What kind of trickery is this? Where am I?"

The darkness and silence offered no clue. All he had been able to remember was light—vicious, penetrating light, raw and pure as liquid. No, more than liquid. Fire. Fire that burned through you until you screamed to be taken away. All he had wanted at that moment was to get away.

Then there had been that voice. High. Omnipotent. The words had flashed like lightning, each one belting him like a boxer's gloved fist. Jeremiah had tried to run. For an endless moment, he was held in place. Finally, he was cast out.

Cast out? he mused.

A hollow yearning pulled at his belly. "I suppose the food in this place is as strange as everything else."

Where could I go to find out?

He moved about, perhaps for an hour—or what seemed like it. But nothing changed, except his now ravenous appetite. His mouth felt drier each moment.

Why am I burning? How can I feel flames without their causing light? That desert was bright . . .

During the war, his platoon had run out of water. Jeremiah remembered maddening thirst, lying on the sand, panting. Mercilessly, the sun had hammered his forehead. His body had screamed for water. Every pore had felt like fire.

Then they had found the sea. It had been all he could do to crawl. Others had walked as he inched his way. They had drunk as he struggled on. And they had died, their stomachs full of saltwater. But he had lain helpless, like now.

Can't lie down, can't eat, can't even scratch my nose. Tears slid down his face. But as hard as he tried, he couldn't wipe them away.

"Answer me! Who are You? Where am I? Answer me!"

The darkness engulfed him, passive and silent. He found himself soothing his conscience. *That's it. Make yourself laugh. You'll snap out of this.*

He began telling himself a joke. But a strange thing happened. He couldn't recall the punch line. The more he thought about it, the more agitated he became. He began going through the alphabet, trying each letter to see if the word began with it. He couldn't remember at all. The punch line was gone.

Something else came to mind—sex. He tried to catch himself. *Don't think of it, or you'll be in the same fix as with the thirst and hunger.*

But it was all there in his mind. Instantly. The tension mounted. And he had no power to satisfy the craving. The desire only seemed to build. Still, no climax terminated the feelings.

His body didn't even seem to exist. It struck him: "I don't exist!" he yelled. That made him laugh, a bitter, chilling chuckle in the darkness.

In his youth, he had often wrangled with the fanatics about life after death, the deity of Christ, the existence of God, and other "ludicrous subjects," as he had called them. He especially enjoyed trouncing them with his logic. One of his pet theories was nonexistence. "When you die," he'd always told them, "you're gone forever. Poof. Nothingness."

Now he groaned. *How can I not exist? I feel everything, every desire.*

He waited, hoping for an answer. But none came. "Do I exist?" he cried. "At least tell me that."

His desires and feelings of thirst and hunger began accumulating, piling up. Fears, dreams, lusts, the desire for ice cream, the thirst for a sip of whiskey, the desire to play a game—and win! But no satisfaction anywhere.

"Is this hell?" he whimpered. "Is this hell?" He started to laugh. "Hell? What's that? There is no hell." He paused. "And for that matter, there's no God."

But there had been the light and that voice. . . . Jeremiah had bowed before Him, admitting to many deeds. Now it was all coming back. Still, that couldn't have been God.

210

"It was a dream. A nightmare. It'll be over as soon as I wake up." Yet, he wasn't sure.

"Is this hell?" he roared again, trying to lash out into the darkness, to send his voice as far as it would go. "Is this hell?" The roar tore his throat. The sudden pain knocked him back, and he grasped at his neck, trying to calm himself. He felt torn, ripped. He could barely speak. He coughed in the darkness and fought to settle himself.

"Tell me," he rasped. "Tell me, please tell me, at least that! Just tell me, is there a God, and is this hell? I've got to know. At least let me know that."

If I could just hear a voice or feel a touch . . .

"I don't know where I am. I don't know why I'm here. I know absolutely nothing about this place, and yet I'm gritting my teeth, weeping, and sweating . . . "

My throat is on fire. I thirst. I hunger. I lust. What is it? What is going on? What has happened?

He remembered the cold, harsh words of the voice. "Depart from Me, you who practice wickedness."

"Is that it?" The question died on his lips. "Have I been wrong all along? Am I really lost?"

It couldn't have been Him. Not Him. God? God Almighty?

"What about my profession of faith?" he yelled. "I walked the aisle and prayed the prayer. The preacher said I was a Christian. Everyone was weeping and congratulating my wife."

He paused and waited. It occurred to him that he should be brutally honest about it. Maybe that was the key. "All right, I did it just to please my wife. But I did everything they said." He grew hopeful. He'd just discovered an ace in his pocket. "Ha!" he challenged, "What about that? I did everything they said."

He waited. He listened. His sense of expectation rose, the way you feel when you expect a phone call any minute. But the phone didn't ring.

He wrung his hands and strained toward the darkness. He turned his head, expecting some acknowledgment. "I suppose You won't even answer that," he said mockingly. "Well, I don't care. You've put me here, and I'm going to curse You and hate You as long as I can.

211

"I curse Your name, God, and Your 'wonderful' justice. I hate You and Your stupid little Book and Your Son who died. I'm going to hate You as long as I'm here. Until You let me out, I'll hate You and loathe You. Hear that? You're nothing to me, God. Nothing. The major Nothing of the universe!" Jeremiah paused for effect.

I'm screaming against my own air. I can't do anything to Him. Nothing.

He made another disturbing discovery. His hatred began to coil up within him, ready to spring. Burning malice and anger flooded his being, like in the old days when someone spoke to him of "his soul." Yet there was nowhere to direct his wrath—except within. Terror gripped him. *It's impossible. Preposterous. But I can't end it.*

"Maybe it will end," he murmured. "Maybe it's just for a little while. Like purgatory." He'd heard of that. Laughed at it. Maybe that was where he was. Being purged.

But nothing was going out of him. Rather, everything twisted up inside him and mounted. He wasn't being purged. He was being deluged, filled, readied to explode, yet he found no release.

Something new hit him so fiercely it almost took his breath. "How long do I have to wait?" he cried. "How long? There has to be an end. All things end sooner or later. Please tell me—how long?"

Immediately, he remembered the voice, "Depart from Me!" Had it said "forever"?

The blackness was immense and the silence vast as a cindered landscape.

How can it be? The silence is the worst. No one here. No friend. No enemy. No one to talk to. No one to curse or counsel or tell off. No one. Nothing!

"You've got to tell me that," he cried again. "How long does this last? Please say it. Anything. Ten years? A hundred? Even a million? Just let me know how long."

He remembered the voice's words, how they echoed as he was carried out. "Forever! Forever! Forever!"

Jeremiah swallowed and closed his eyes. "No! It can't be. Not forever! Please, it has to be less than that. I can stand anything if I know how long. How long will this be? Tell me. Please have that much mercy!"

He fought back the tears. "I won't cry," he said. "I won't. I won't give them that."

He swung around. "Please, I can't stand it. I didn't know it would be like this. Please. Have mercy. Please, have a little mercy."

The moment he said "mercy" a new revulsion came over him. Mercy? *I never asked for mercy in my life, and I'm not starting now, not even here.*

He remembered what he'd said to the voice, to God. "Take Your mercy, God, and Your world, too. Take it all. I don't need it. I don't want You or Your mercy, or anything of Yours. I just want to get out of here."

What had He said? "So be it. You have said so by your own lips."

So be it! No, it can't be. This can't be the end.

Jeremiah fought to push his thoughts away. But they were screaming inside him. *Just a drop of water! Just a piece of bread! Just a friend! Just someone to talk to! Please!* He waited. Something had to happen.

Nothing did. It was as silent and burning as ever. A rage flooded through him like the flames of a bonfire. "Take Your food and Your water and Your people and shove it, God! I don't want any of it. Hear me? Do You hear me? I hate You! How do You like that? Do You feel it? Does it make You want to cry?" He waited. But nothing changed. Only his desires, the raging thirst, and the burning in his belly seemed to increase.

"I can't get to Him," he moaned. "I can't touch Him." He fought to think. What could he do? How could he get back at God? How could he hurt Him?

But then something even stranger happened. As his anger became clearer, he realized the only place he could direct it was at himself. He could now hurt no one in existence but himself. Not his wife. Not his children. Not his boss. No one. No one anywhere.

He gasped and tried to loosen the tight feeling around his neck, the pain he always got when he was terrifically afraid. The tightening only increased. He twisted around, shaking his fist and gnashing his teeth.

Gnashing their teeth. Wasn't that what the Bible said? The thought struck him deeply. He was in hell. This was the end. This was his end. All those elaborate plans, and he had come to this.

But I'll get out! I'll find some way. I've always found a way! He waited. Still nothing changed. Only his jaw pained now, and the tightness around his neck and the fire in his gut seemed to increase.

Suddenly, he screamed, "I hate You, God! Take that! I don't care how long it takes down here. I'll wait You out, God. Hear me? I'll wait longer than You. I'll beat You at Your own game, God!"

The darkness and silence only seemed heavier, darker, quieter.

God has condemned me—forever. I thought it was a weakling's religion, a bunch of nonsense. He remembered all the services he had attended, all the times his pastor had spoken to him, all the times his wife had prayed and pleaded.

"Why didn't I believe?" he shouted. "Was I insane?"

His thoughts seemed to shout back: *Because you thought it was nonsense. Remember? Boring. An irritation you could live without. Remember?*

Jeremiah looked up, straining his neck. "Is there no hope?"

The unquenchable desires within him began another rampage. He smelled smoke, fire. "Brimstone," he murmured. "It's brimstone." It burned inside him, scorching his soul.

"That's where I am, aren't I? Aren't I, God?"

He thought back through his life about everything he'd ever done. Nothing in life was like this. The words came back to him. *Forever! Forever! FOREVER!*

He fought to think of some way out, some way beyond. There had always been hope back on earth. Hope for a better day. For change. For something to give way. Here was nothing but darkness, silence, and internal fire.

He had to find hope, something that spoke inside him, that calmed his soul. But inside he knew. He had even agreed with Him. The punishment was just. In fact, he had wanted it—to get back, to punish God, to hurt Him. But more than anything he wanted to get away from that light, that burning, searing light.

He shook his fist and snarled. The burning raged on. He fought for control. He fought to hold back his feelings. He shrieked, "Why didn't I believe? Why didn't I trust Him?"

He knew the answer. It coiled and burned and raged within him. *Because I hated Him and His rules and His people and His book. I hated everything about Him. And why?*

There was no good reason. No good reason! He was good. He was just. He was kind. He offered me every opportunity. And I rejected Him. For no good reason. I just did.

As he thought, something strangled Jeremiah. *I've been a fool. A complete fool. I blew everything. And now I'm lost. Forever!*

He gasped. He closed his eyes and tried to think. But there was no more thinking. It was over.

Weakly, quietly it started. But it began to build. Higher, higher, stronger, tearing through his whole body, soul, and mind. His throat ripped and burned, his whole body shook, and his mind burned with pain and fire. Soon he could hear nothing but himself—the plaintive, broken wail of the damned.

27
The Beggar's Request

Once a great king invited all to come to his kingdom and find an answer to every need. From a long way off, Zebedee the lame beggar heard this news and decided he would journey to find the king and perhaps cease to be a beggar or lame.

Zebedee set off, and on the way he asked travelers if they'd heard of the king and knew anything of his gifts and power. Some travelers told him they'd heard of this king, but they regarded it as rumor and had never tried to find him. Others reported that the story was basically true in its primitive elements, but when they scrutinized it closely they'd found that most of the people who made the great reports tended to exaggerate and augment the king's abilities till they appeared far greater than they really were.

After many such encounters, Zebedee was ready to turn back. Then he chanced upon Libnah, a young man of fair complexion and bright eyes. Libnah came beaming down the road, and Zebedee stopped him. "Do you know anything about the great king who gives riches to the poor, sight to the blind, and hope to the suffering?"

Libnah answered, "I have come from precisely that place, and I would be quite glad to tell you all about it." He proceeded to tell Zebedee his tale of dire woe and destruction so awful that at one point Libnah despaired of life itself. But he had gone to the king for sustenance, and the king had given him a thousand gold pieces. With that in hand, Libnah had gotten his family out of debt, himself a new vocation, and a total change of heart about life. He had become happy.

Zebedee was amazed and thanked Libnah for his words. He asked, "Many have said other things—the king is a fake, the king is a rumor, and so on—how do I know what you say is true?"

"Look at me," said Libnah. "Why would I exalt a rumor? Why would I praise a fake? Here, take a gold piece yourself."

He flipped Zebedee one of the pieces of gold that he had in his purse. "Would I be willing to part with my money if I had not learned from the king to be generous?"

Zebedee smiled. He knew instantly that it had to be true, for few people exalted or praised a figment of their imagination, except madmen, and Libnah was no madman. So Zebedee thanked him and sped on toward the king's realm, resolving that he would request a bag of riches from the king as Libnah had done.

He continued to ply travelers for news. Many still disdained the king, said the journey was too far or claimed that they already had their needs met. But Zebedee chanced upon another authentic believer, this time a man who walked jauntily up the road with a majestic staff.

"Ho!" cried Zebedee. "Know you anything of the king who gives riches to the poor, sight to the blind, and hope to the suffering?"

"Absolutely," said the man, whose name was Larkson. "I have just come from his kingdom and have been wondrously healed of a terrible malady. I see that you are lame, but you can be sure that with the king you will find new health and never be lame again."

Larkson went on to describe a tale of pain and hurt that made Zebedee's eyes tear. But he had journeyed to the king and found healing from his terrible leprosy. "And as you can see," he said, extending his hands and pulling up his pant leg, "I am completely healed."

Zebedee again rejoiced, but he wanted to make sure, so he said, "How can I be convinced that what you say is true?"

Larkson laughed. "Would I show you a leg that was leprous? Would I extend my hand if the skin was white with disease? Here, grasp my arm."

Zebedee grasped it.

"Do you feel the strength in it? That is because of the king. Why would I forge lies about him if I had done these things myself? For who among men does not love to tell of his own doings?"

So Zebedee believed once again and decided that when he reached the king he would not only ask for riches but for healing as well.

Again, he crossed paths with many who were skeptical and even those who fiercely opposed what the king had promised. But Zebedee chanced upon a man whose smile shed sunlight on all he passed. He stopped the man and asked, "How is it, sir, that you smile with such freedom, and your joy seems to run deep as the heart?"

The man, whose name was Plink, didn't hesitate. "It is because the king has refreshed my soul, rid me of despair, and made me a new man through and through."

Plink went on to tell a story of such woe that Zebedee nearly fell to the ground in shock. When he learned how the king had given Plink new hope after suffering many evils, from personal pain to loss of relatives to the execution of a son for false crimes, he rejoiced and shook Plink's hand joyously. Still, he wondered if all that Plink said was true, and he said, "How can I be sure that what you say happened—truly happened?"

Plink said, "If I had done it myself, I would boast in myself. If my joy was from my own heart, it would certainly be sorrow. As it is, the king has touched my heart and changed me. What I was, I no longer am, and what I could be, I have become—because of the king. Here, let me take you to my breast and assure you that I would never have loved another if I had first not felt the king's love." With that, Plink hugged Zebedee to his breast, and the two men wept for joy.

"I must speed on, then, and receive from this king what he will give," said Zebedee, and they parted.

As he journeyed, hobbling on his crutch, with only a piece of gold to his name and the remembrance of love in his heart, Zebedee thought about what he would ask from the king. "First, hope in despair, as Plink has found. Then healing of my lame leg. And finally, riches. What else might I ask of such a wondrous king?"

As he drew closer to the castle of the king, he met more and more people who had received his great gifts. Blind men who saw. Deaf women who could hear. The demon-possessed set free. Poor children with new clothes and brightly colored aprons. Mothers who smiled and rejoiced in new riches and new hope.

Zebedee thought about all this bounty and began to realize he wanted something far more than healing, new clothing, riches, and hope. He wasn't sure what it was. But he knew it would come to him in time.

At last he stood at the castle gate. The guard let him in and took him to the throne room of the king. There was a long line, and the king dispensed his gifts to each supplicant as they came to him. Zebedee watched in wonder as each person received precisely what he or she wanted and needed.

He noticed something else. The king's face, though joyous and kind, was creased with care. "He must be one who feels deeply," Zebedee murmured to himself as he watched.

He noticed also that the king listened intently to each person, and as he came closer to the front, he said to himself, "He must be one who sees deeply."

He continued to watch and noted that the king, in each case, asked questions that were so exact and plunged to the heart of the matter so quickly that Zebedee found himself saying, "He must be one who knows the heart and condition of man well, and that must give him great pain. He must be one who thinks deeply."

Finally, there were only a few people ahead of him, and Zebedee watched as the king transformed a forlorn family from a band of beggars to a passel of princes. Even as the king spoke, Zebedee could see the power go out of him. He murmured, "He must be one who loves deeply."

Then it was his turn. The king looked him in the eye and said, "And what may I do for you, friend?"

The way he said "friend" was so genuine and perfect that Zebedee almost shrank into his cloak, ashamed to ask for such small things for himself. What was it that he wanted, truly wanted, more than all the rest? He still wasn't sure.

"O king," he said, "I have come from miles away, and I have heard many stories—great and wondrous stories. I spoke to one young man, Libnah..."

"Yes," the king said with a nod. "I remember him. A decent young man but poor."

"Yes!" said Zebedee, surprised. "And I thought that I would ask you for some of the same riches. You would give me this?"

The king nodded. "Of course. I have much, and you have so little. I can give you all you desire."

Zebedee cleared his throat and said, "But as I traveled, I realized I wanted something more. I met Larkson, whom you healed from leprosy."

"Yes, he was a bold man, as I recall," said the king. "A joyous man. I liked him."

Zebedee almost choked with amazement. But he went on, "You would heal me from my lameness?"

"Yes," said the king. "I have many cures, and this one is not difficult."

Zebedee said, "And then I met Plink..."

The king smiled with a look of pain in his eyes. "In such despair, even I thought I could not help him. But somehow..."

"You did!" said Zebedee, hardly able to catch his breath.

The king laughed. "You have met many good and kind people whom I love. So what is your request?"

Zebedee still couldn't think beyond his own immediate needs. He said, "Your Majesty, I would like gold to pay my debts and provide for my family, healing from my lameness, and the joy of a hope certain to come to pass."

The king nodded. "It is done," he said. Immediately, Zebedee straightened up, his lameness gone. A bag of gold lay at his feet. And his heart was full to bursting. He thanked the king and turned to go. The next man and his family came up and began their request.

Suddenly, Zebedee turned around. He knew now what he wanted. "Sire!"

The king looked at him and motioned to the others to be silent. "Yes?"

Zebedee was almost afraid to speak. But he mustered the courage. He wasn't sure if what he wanted was possible. "Sire, all this I will give back, if you will grant me one request."

The king shook his head. "You need give nothing back. What is your request?"

Zebedee swallowed and fought to frame his words. There was no better way than a simple petition. "Your Majesty, please understand, I'm a humble man. I have never had much, and I don't ask much—even though you have given me all this. But if you will grant me this one request, I know I shall have a satisfaction that shall last all my life."

The king smiled. "And what is it, my son?"

Zebedee looked down at his feet and at the bag of gold. He held his breath. What if his request were refused? Still, he had to ask. All the court was deadly quiet. He looked up into the king's deep, gray eyes. "Your Majesty, I want to be with you, to know you, to be your friend."

The courtroom froze, dumbstruck. No one had ever heard of such a request. The king himself seemed amazed and gazed at Zebedee a long time. He seemed to be struggling with something deep inside himself. Then he said, "Of all the thousands who have come to me, none has ever made such a request."

Zebedee swallowed and bowed his head. "I would exchange it all to be near you, Sire."

The king's eyes were grave. A great tear formed in his eye and fell onto a crease in his robe. Then he spoke. "Such great faith I have not found with anyone in my kingdom! I have given great gifts to many. But you, Zebedee, have given a gift to me." He rose from his throne and walked over to Zebedee, and embraced him. Together they wept.

The king said, "I have waited for this moment for many years."

221

Zebedee bowed. The king smiled, putting his arm on Zebedee's shoulder. "It is done. You and your family shall be with me. As long as I reign." Tears welled into Zebedee's eyes. He bowed again before his master.

28
Only the Beginning

I remembered everything. We met Him in the air, as it had been written. At the time, it had seemed impossible that such a prophecy could be fulfilled so exactly. But when it happened, everything became clear in an instant. It was as it had been written all along. Nothing had been left to chance or misinterpretation.

Now we were to stand before Him. This moment, this day, had always seemed so distant, so far away. But now here I was. All of us, gathered. White robes like light. Faces beautiful and young. Everyone delighted, ebullient, secure.

But I was afraid. What would He say about me? What *could* He say?

All my life, I'd known the words. "He will repay everyone according to his deeds." "We must all stand before the judgment seat." "He will recompense us for our deeds in the body, according to what we have done, whether good or bad."

I'd always thought . . .

What does it matter what I had thought? This was reality. The real thing. There was no hiding now, no going back, no changes to make.

I knew very well what would happen, or, should I say, could happen. That passage in Corinthians—he shall escape "as through fire." That was me. I might as well not try to hide it. Everything would be burned up, nothing left worthy of reward.

After all, what is a salesman? What is the machinery industry? What was being a husband and father? Anybody can do those things.

But deep down, I wished I'd done something grand. Like those early Fathers. "The golden-throated." Who was he? Chrysostom? Or one of the great monks. Or Augustine, Thomas Aquinas, Luther, Calvin, Zwingli. Wesley, Whitefield, Spurgeon. I had heard about them. Pastors I had sat under referred to them all the time. Joan of Arc, Tyndale, Hus. History blazed with them like great bolts of lightning upon the pages of writ.

Next to them, who was I?

I tried not to feel sorry for myself. In fact, I couldn't. All I could feel was a vague sense of regret. At one time I had sensed a call, at least I thought I had. But circumstances had prevented . . .

No, I couldn't even use that excuse. Things had just never worked out the way I'd hoped. I had been afraid mainly, and young. Then middle-aged. Then old. Then too late.

I tried to do things. But I hadn't been good at them. Teaching in the Sunday school, what was that? None of my students went on to be great pastors or teachers. At least none that I knew.

Serving on the deacon board? I had been asked several times. But I'd never felt qualified. Who was I? Just a salesman. I knew I did things I didn't like. I always confessed them and tried to make them right. But it never endeared me to the board of deacons.

Please understand. I'm not trying to make you feel sorry for me. I just didn't see what I'd amounted to. I did decent work. I had tried to be honest. When I hedged, I always tried to make it right. I sold a good product: printing machinery. I advanced in my company. I gave people a fair shake.

But who didn't try to do that? It had little to do with being a Christian. I suppose in a way I'd done it just to make sure nothing came back to me. In that industry, things had a way of hitting you over the head a year or two down the road, if you weren't straight with people. But there had been lots of men who had nothing to do with Jesus who had done the same. What did that merit?

I hadn't been anything but a very average guy. Man, I hated saying it. It sounded so stupid. "Pretty average guy." Maybe "less than average" was a better description.

But here it was now. The judgment. Everything accounted for. Standing before Him. What was I supposed to say: "Hey, I can't wait till you make me Your right hand man, Lord"? I didn't even lead many people to Christ. I could count on my left hand the number of people that I knew had stuck with Him.

That bothered me a lot, too. I had passed out tracts at times. I told people what I believed. I "witnessed," as we had called it in my age. But I never saw much fruit. Certainly not the "thirty-fold, sixty-fold, or a hundred-fold" that Jesus spoke about. I could remember one, maybe two folks. But I'd lost touch with them. I didn't even know where they ended up.

I was beginning to feel worse and worse. Even with a new body and a sense of perfection, I felt a little sick. What was He going to say? "Glad to have you here, Mr. Colter. Have a good eternity!"

How much could He sugarcoat a below-average life? Well, maybe it hadn't been below average. Was that mock humility? I mean, I had had a good life. A decent life. I had enjoyed it. I liked things like church and worship and visiting people and trying to teach. I had even liked reading the Bible and praying. I wasn't any Holy Joe, but I did have something of a "spiritual walk," as we called it.

In a way, though, I almost wished He would simply pass over me. Like when the whole team wins the trophy, but no one is singled out for special mention. But all I really was hoping for was no reprimands. No angry exposures.

But everyone would have a chance to stand up here. Each of us would stand before the Bema.

It was almost funny. Remember how we used to try to "say something nice" about someone? I remember my dad telling us kids, "If you don't have something good to say, don't say it." A lot of times, though, you'd exaggerate or make up something to make a friend feel good, even though you knew what you said was only half true.

But I knew He wouldn't do that. He was holy, perfect, just. He couldn't make things up about me or anyone else just to make me feel good. Doing that always had a negative kick-back anyway. Sooner or later you realized it was all just flattery, and you lost respect for the person who did it. I knew one thing: He wouldn't make me lose respect for Him.

What *would* He come up with? Frankly, I couldn't think of a thing. I had never got my name in the paper, except once as a Little League manager of my son's team. And I never wrote a book or sang a solo or preached a great sermon or even discipled someone who went on to serve the Lord in great and significant ways. The people I had discipled, well, they never did much better than me. They just lived, so far as I could tell, decent, quiet lives with few or no big moments. Anyway, what was the point of flagellating myself? I'd just have to take what came. "Chin up," my mom always said.

She was there, you know. I honestly hadn't thought she would be. But I was overjoyed. All those years of lambasting her with the gospel. And all along she'd believed. Not quite like me, but she had believed, and that satisfied Him.

Dad, too. And my sister and brother and members of their families. I had never thought it could be true. I had always been caught up in certain rather narrow interpretations of things. But they all had believed. They hadn't had the kind of "lightning bolt," born-again experience I had had, so I'd always thought that meant they didn't really have faith. But they did.

My three kids were there, too. And my wife. I don't know what I would have done if they hadn't made it. I had been confident they would, of course, because I knew they believed. But there were always doubts.

And I was there! Even if He couldn't honestly say, "Well done," I was still there. I was part of His kingdom forever and ever. My loved ones were there. Most of them. And it would never end. There was plenty of rejoicing in that.

And then it began. He called us by name and each one came forward.

It was astonishing. I wasn't bored or tired for a moment. He stood each one before the rest of us. We could see right into that person; his heart was revealed before us. We saw all that he or she had done. We went right on through the ages, from the beginning of time.

In this place there was no sense of time. You could concentrate completely on what was happening around you without forgetting what had gone before or what was coming after. I'm sure it all took several years in earth time, although there was no way to tell. And it didn't matter.

I was looking forward to the twentieth century. I had some things to say about people I had known. I had already had opportunities to talk about people throughout history who had had special ministries in my life. I got to thank Habakkuk and Elijah and Abraham—all of them. Paul, Peter, James. I was able to tell them how reading things from their writings had influenced me. I remarked on things I'd read from Martin Luther and Calvin and Wesley. It was marvelous, thanking and praising those people in person. All of them were rewarded.

He Himself spoke. So many "well dones." So many accolades.

I almost wished I had been some of those people. They'd done so much. But I would be content, I knew, with whatever happened to me, even if it were little. There were a few, yes, a very few, who seemed to "escape so as through fire." But even in their cases . . .

It choked me up to think of it because I knew I might be one of them. So I didn't want to sound hard or disappointed when it happened to me. I just wished . . .

I had to make myself stop saying that! Whatever happened to me happened. It was a strange feeling. On the one hand, I longed that everyone be rewarded well. Yet, when it came to myself, I had no idea what He might say. The suspense was almost murderous.

Each time before He spoke, He gave the whole group a chance to tell and bear witness to what the person on the judgment seat had done. It was amazing, the things that were said. Words, kindnesses, good deeds, thanks, praise. Everything was remembered. For some of them—such as Paul and Peter—the talk went on and on until He Himself pronounced a judgment and gave the reward. Yet, many received rewards similar to both Paul's and Peter's. I almost began to hope that He might find something about me.

He took each of us by order of birth and gave everyone a chance to speak. Then He opened the book—their book, the one on each of their lives—passed it through the fire, and whatever gold, silver, and precious stones were upon it He gave to the subject as part of his or her reward. There were all sorts of crowns, the hidden manna, the white stone, and many other honors. Each one was individual and complete. At the end, everyone agreed that His judgment was perfect.

Frankly, I never wanted it to end. Everyone was excited and happy. You just wanted the person up there to do well and to receive a just reward. You were rooting for everyone. When He did pronounce His judgment, you knew it was right and exact, and you took everything in. I trusted Him. I knew He'd bring it all out right.

It was a blur, yet everyone's deeds and face were imprinted on my mind. When I met them personally later, I knew I'd remember everything they'd been commended for and even praise them for it.

Then He came to the year of my birth, 1950.

It would be my turn soon. What would He say? What could He say? I was practically jumping in place. I felt like a schoolkid waiting for his report card and not being sure whether he'd get an F or an A or something in between. Why was I so unsure?

Then He spoke my name.

I wove my way through the crowd to the Bema. He motioned to me to stand before Him. He was so august. Like light. There was a warmth about Him, a kindness. It filled me and made me feel confident. Love—that was it. He loved me! I could feel His love holding me and strengthening me.

He asked the crowd if anyone wanted to speak. My son stepped forward first. "There are so many things, Lord."

"Tell them all," He said.

I was astonished. We had had some bitter times on earth.

But he began. "I remember his playing with me, Lord. Piggyback rides. Singing songs in the car. Fun. He made life fun. And he told me about You." He recounted all sorts of deeds. I was amazed and grateful. These were the things he remembered?

My wife said she had always loved the way I held her, even when I was tired and wanted to go to sleep. She spoke of how I gave her money to buy groceries and clothing with a smile and no resentment. She seemed to go on and on. A lump formed in my throat, and I fought to control my tears. Her face shone like the sun. I was so thankful He had given her to me.

There were others who told of my teaching them in church, a Bible story which had stuck in their mind and influenced them later in life. One boy said, "He told a story one time in Sunday school about Zaccheus's giving his money back to the poor. Later in life it motivated me to help some homeless people."

My mouth dropped open. He remembered that? I didn't even remember that!

Johnny Martin—I'd taught him to throw a ball. Bill Briggs, a fellow salesman—I'd been patient training him, and he'd come to Christ years after he left our company. Doris Liston—my strong singing in church one Sunday had encouraged her. It went on and on. Most of the time I was in tears. I couldn't believe it.

A lady named Grace Schwartz had broken down on the road with a flat tire, and I had fixed it. I hadn't even known she was a Christian. I had witnessed to her, sort of, but she was bitter at the time about problems in her marriage and didn't tell me. She said my words had reminded her of the need to walk with Jesus again.

There was a boy, now a man, from my Little League team—Casey Szabo—who said I had encouraged him and given him a Bible verse. Even though he wasn't a believer at the time, it had come into his mind years later when he did believe.

The time I'd prayed for a friend during a funeral.

The time I'd turned off a leaky faucet in the company bathroom because I thought the Lord would be pleased.

The time I talked in church about the need to give sacrificially.

I'd forgotten them all. They seemed so insignificant. But He had said that anything done in His name would last. And it did.

It seemed that it would never stop. Every impression, every word—there were thousands of them—stitched itself into my heart.

Then the Lord Himself put the book in the fire. And suddenly there was gold, silver, and jewels. So many pieces I couldn't count them. Each one a remembrance of a deed, a word, a thought, a prayer. They were all remembered. Every one.

And He spoke. He reminded me that I had practiced biblical principles in my work. He recounted that nearly every day I had refused to lie or cheat or steal. That I had been honest, worked hard, and given a good day's work to my employer. I hadn't even known if it mattered.

He spoke of how I had worked to be a good husband, listening to my wife, changing, growing, learning, responding to her needs. He pointed out that I had stuck by her even when there were problems that could have ended in divorce. He remembered that I had tried to teach the family the Bible and had applied its principles. Even though He had not given me gifts in the area of teaching or speaking, He said I had tried and had done well.

He reminded me of how I labored to be a good father. He brought out deeds of gentleness and patience that even my children didn't remember. Every time I had prayed in the car for someone, He pointed the answer out, and sometimes people stood and thanked me for my deed.

He showed me the accounting books of my giving to organizations and to the church. Missionaries, pastors, people all over the world stood—from Nigeria and China and Israel, places I knew little about and had never visited—and praised me for my deeds to them, although neither they nor I had known anything about them.

It went on and on. He moved on through my life, picking out each episode of good, showing who had benefited. There

230

were people who had become Christians through the smallest particles of my influence—a kind word, a tract, a prayer in passing.

There were people that I'd prayed for while standing in supermarket lines. They'd become Christians, sometimes years later. He had them all stand. They thanked me and acknowledged my help.

He spoke of others who were simply touched by my presence. He showed how many people in the gathering had been influenced by my family's saying grace in restaurants. Often at the time, I had been vaguely uneasy. But He showed that some of those people were moved toward faith by those small acts.

Then He asked all the people to stand who had been in some way influenced by something I had done—whether it was a prayer for a missionary in Europe or a small gift to an organization in Los Angeles. All of it was connected. I could not count the number of people who stood and cheered and thanked me.

I couldn't stop feeling choked up. The things I had done—the little things I considered so small and unimportant—had had these far-reaching effects?

Finally, after it was all done, He stood to speak. "John," He said, "look at Me."

I looked into His eyes. It was the most hallowed, cleansing, thrilling moment of my life. As I looked at Him, I saw His heart. It was revealed in that blinding moment. I saw who He was and how He had loved me. I knew then that my God had loved me from all eternity and that I had been in His heart before I was even conceived in my mother's womb. I knew that He would never leave me and had been with me through every experience. I knew that He had ordered every detail of my life to bring me to this moment of triumph. And I saw that long ago He had planned every opportunity for a good deed in advance so that when I came to this moment there would be much to reward me for.

I knew it all in that instant. And in that instant I loved Him as I had never loved Him.

231

He spoke, His eyes shining and true. "John, you have done all that I planned. You have done many good works in My name. You have touched the lives of thousands. Well done, good and faithful servant. You will sit with Me and rule with Me on My throne. I welcome you into the joy of your Father."

He embraced me, and in that moment, the fear and doubt fell away forever. Then He presented me to the gathering. "Welcome John Colter into the eternal bliss and reward of his Lord."

The cheering never seemed to stop. And it was only the beginning.